PRIMARY FOUNDATIONS

Physical education

AGES 9-11

Pauline Boorman
and Bob Bellew

CONTENTS

Authors
Pauline Boorman
and Bob Bellew

Editor
Simon Tomlin

Assistant editor
Roanne Davis

Series designer
Lynne Joesbury

Designer
Rachel Warner

Illustrations
Beverly Curl

Cover photograph
Martyn Chillmaid

**Published by
Scholastic Ltd,**
Villiers House,
Clarendon Avenue,
Leamington Spa,
Warwickshire
CV32 5PR
**Printed by Bell & Bain
Ltd, Glasgow**
Text © Pauline Boorman
and Bob Bellew
© 2001
Scholastic Ltd

2 3 4 5 6 7 8 9 0
2 3 4 5 6 7 8 9 0

British Library Cataloguing-in-Publication Data
A catalogue record for this book is available from
the British Library.

ISBN 0-439-01843-9

The right of Pauline Boorman and Bob Bellew to be identified as the Authors of this work has been asserted
by them in accordance with the Copyright, Designs and Patents Act 1988.

Introduction

The importance of physical education

'Physical Education develops pupils' physical competence and confidence, and their ability to use these to perform in a range of activities. It promotes physical skilfulness, physical development and a knowledge of the body in action. It provides opportunities for pupils to be creative, competitive and to face challenges as individuals and in groups and teams. It promotes positive attitudes towards active and healthy lifestyles. Pupils learn how to plan, perform and evaluate actions, ideas and performances to improve their aptitudes, abilities and preferences, and make choices about how to get involved in lifelong physical activity.' (*The National Curriculum Handbook for Primary Teachers in England: Key Stages 1 and 2*, DfEE/QCA).

At a time when there are real concerns over the low levels of physical activity amongst British school children, when children are becoming heavier and fatter and are leading increasingly sedentary lifestyles, this statement highlights the important contribution of PE, not only to promoting healthy lifestyles but to the whole developmental process.

Movement is probably the most natural and spontaneous learning medium for children. It capitalises on their inherent playful enthusiasm for active involvement in everything around them. It is indeed the essence of childhood and as such is an essential entitlement for all children and an integral part of a broad, balanced curriculum. Schools alone cannot meet the exercise needs of children, but they do have a responsibility to broaden and extend their physical experiences in a variety of contexts (indoors and outdoors, individually and with others, with a variety of equipment) and to help them to move safely, efficiently, imaginatively and with increasing control.

Movement involves three very different but complementary facets of learning: learning how to move, learning through movement and learning about movement.

Learning how to move

The development of physical literacy enables children to manage the everyday demands of living: to be co-ordinated and skilful, creative and expressive, sensitive and energetic in a variety of gross and fine motor activities. In every lesson, all children should have as much opportunity, experience and practice to develop their confidence and competence in these areas as possible.

It is the physical nature of this mode of learning that gives it its distinct identity and makes it unique in the school situation in the sense of being only specifically addressed in physical education. Yet its impact on all other areas of development on the whole learning process, as recent brain studies suggest, can be inestimable (sitting still is one of the more refined of physical skills).

Learning through movement

Links with other areas of the curriculum

We all learn by doing, and for young children particularly, practical experience is an essential ingredient for involvement, assimilation and understanding and often motivation. Through involvement in physical activities, children are presented with many opportunities to think, plan, remember, discuss, assess and solve problems, make decisions and use their judgement. These are skills that are relevant across the curriculum.

There are many ways of using movement as a way of extending, for example, mathematical, literacy, scientific or geographical understanding. It is essential, however, that this is not done in artificial or contrived ways, but in ways that genuinely contribute to understanding in other areas.

Links with personal and social education

Movement also has the potential for providing, extending and enhancing many activities that make demands on children's personal and social capabilities, for example in situations that call for interaction, sharing, taking turns, leading and following, collaboration, negotiation, responsibility and use of language. We know that physical activity affects feelings of well-being in a broader sense, but

activities that involve children in working in a group or team are not in themselves sufficient to ensure that children work effectively together. Children need to be helped in their interactions in ways that build on their sense of achievement and develop their self-esteem. It is important to develop their confidence and sense of achievement through varied and enjoyable practical activities.

Links with literacy and language
Throughout each unit of work, children are encouraged to listen and respond to others and to describe, explain and talk about their ideas and activities using appropriate language and some specialist vocabulary. It should be remembered, however, that physical education is primarily about doing, and opportunities for discussion should be brief and purposeful or take place primarily in the classroom, otherwise children might get bored, cold and restless.

Links with numeracy and science
The activities suggested in this book provide ideas for developing an understanding of shape, space and measures in a practical context, experiencing and coming to understand forces and motion in a meaningful way and developing an understanding of the effect of exercise on the body.

Learning about movement
With the current concerns about sedentary lifestyles, increasing obesity and the evidence of many hypokinetic diseases beginning in childhood, there are obvious implications for the primary teacher. The most important aspect of this focus on the body, and how it works, is the notion of a developing health awareness. The aspects particularly highlighted in the National Curriculum are each child's knowledge and understanding of fitness and health and of the effects of physical exercise on their bodies. By raising awareness of the role of physical activity in their lives and helping children towards feelings of satisfaction, exhilaration and fun derived from their sense of progress and achievement in physical education, it is hoped that these activities will encourage participation in the full sense of the word (thinking and doing) and that children can be helped to develop positive attitudes and a commitment to physical activity; to make reasoned, informed and healthy lifestyle choices.

About *Primary Foundations PE*
Through activities in dance, gymnastics, games, athletics, outdoor and adventurous activities and swimming, this book attempts to address the requirements of the curriculum and involve children in movement in a meaningful and practical way, in enjoyable and purposeful physical activity.

The units suggest ideas and detail ways in which practical activities can be developed and enhanced within a unit of work or series of lessons.

For each of the core areas of PE (games, dance and gymnastics), aspects are developed in greater depth (two for dance and gym, five for games). The chapters suggest alternative activities or develop those outlined in the QCA schemes. One unit for swimming, for those schools that choose to teach it during this phase of Key Stage 2, and one unit each of athletics and outdoor and adventurous activities are also included. Each unit of work can be used to plan half a term's work for the area it covers: 30–45 minutes of activity per lesson. The units:
● provide a basis for developing and extending physical literacy… enhancing each child's movement repertoire and vocabulary in the core areas
● use a combination of exploratory, suggested, guided and directed activities to enable children to practise and develop their skills
● provide links with other areas of the curriculum.

It is important that the ideas given are seen as example plans. There is a great need for flexibility to suit the particular needs of each class or group. As with other areas of the curriculum, you will need to take account of children's previous experiences, current interests and developmental needs.

You will need to use a range of teaching styles and approaches; balancing activities that may be teacher-directed (as is often necessary at the beginning of a lesson to stimulate and involve the children) with activities in which children explore independently or collaborate with others and work together, gradually taking greater responsibility for their own learning.

The lessons suggested blend together some independent choices and directed activities with some challenges and activities to boost confidence. All have the potential for all sorts of learning through movement if one is open to the possibilities. It is hoped that you will be able to enjoy the activities with the children: observing, encouraging, teaching and monitoring their progress.

National Curriculum

'During Key Stage 2 pupils enjoy being active and using their creativity and imagination in physical activity. They learn new skills, use them in different ways and link them to make action phrases and sequences of movement. They enjoy communicating, collaborating and competing. They develop an understanding of how to succeed in different activities and learn how to evaluate and recognise their success.' (*The National Curriculum Handbook for Primary Teachers in England*, DfEE/QCA)

The activities in this book contribute towards the attainment target that sets out the development of the knowledge, skills and understanding that children of different abilities are expected to have attained by the end of Key Stage 2. The activities are designed to enhance the requirements of the National Curriculum, and provide examples of ways in which the QCA guidelines can be fleshed out.

Acquiring and developing skills
The units will help children to:
- explore ways of using their bodies in different contexts
- repeat skills, actions and ideas with increasing control, co-ordination and understanding
- practise and refine their actions
- manipulate and handle apparatus and equipment
- develop observation and social skills.

Selecting and applying skills, tactics and compositional ideas
Children will be encouraged to prepare and plan for physical activity by:
- choosing, selecting, adapting, varying and modifying actions and ideas
- remembering and linking together
- inventing and creating.

Evaluating and improving performance
Children will be prompted to:
- describe what they have done, what they liked and what they might do differently next time
- observe, analyse and appreciate the movement of others
- talk and think about what they have done and what they have achieved during the lessons.

Knowledge and understanding of fitness and health
Children will learn:
- how important it is to be active
- how to exercise safely, for example why we warm up before activity and cool down afterwards
- a greater awareness of how their bodies feel during different activities.

Encouraging independence and personal responsibility
The activities will help children to increase awareness of themselves and others and the context in which they are working, and develop an awareness of safety.

Inclusion

It is now statutory in physical education to provide effective learning opportunities for all children. Teachers are obliged to:

● consider the full requirements of the inclusion statement when planning for individuals or groups
● take account of children's religious and cultural beliefs and practices, such as allowing leggings for Muslim children but discouraging scarves which can be hazardous
● overcome any potential barriers to learning in physical education (some children may require adapted or alternative activities that have integrity and equivalence to the activities in the programmes of study and that enable children to progress, such as a way of travelling rather than jumping, or using a ball with a bell in it for a child who is partially sighted; specific support to enable them to participate in certain activities or types of movement, such as the buddy system, NSA support person; careful management of their physical regime to allow for specific medical conditions such as asthma and epilepsy)
● consider planning – where a support assistant is assigned to a child then they should be involved in the planning of activities
● in assessment, when children follow adapted or alternative activities, judge against level descriptions made in the context of the activities undertaken by the child.

For all children, there is a great need to recognise effort and progress rather than measure them against predetermined criteria.

Safety

Challenge and adventure are natural aspects of children's play. By their nature, many of the activities are hazardous and involve an element of risk. Such challenges within PE are both stimulating and demanding of each child's initiative, courage and determination, as well as their physical capabilities.

One of the most important priorities is to teach children to recognise and cope with the dangers around them in a constructive and positive way, whether it be raising their awareness of their use of skipping ropes, bats and throwing equipment in a limited space; of others as they move about; sharing the responsibility for using or handling apparatus; or preparing themselves for activity, for going outside, to the swimming pool or further afield. Simple rules can be discussed and established, with the children becoming fully involved in their implementation so they appreciate the need for them.

Trial and error is a necessary part of the learning process, but in the context of physical activity, it can often be a long and painful process. Safety precautions cannot remove all risks, but should eliminate all unnecessary dangers. Every opportunity should be used to help children develop a sense of safety, alerting them to ways in which their actions may impinge upon the safety of others.

The health and safety requirements of the current curriculum are quite general, so it is useful to look back on the more detailed requirements of the NCC Physical Education non-statutory guidance, June 1992, which states that within all activities, at whatever stage, 'pupils should be taught to:

● be concerned with their own and others' safety in all activities undertaken
● lift, carry and place equipment safely
● understand why particular clothing, footwear and protection are worn for different activities
● understand the safety risks of wearing inappropriate clothing, footwear and jewellery
● respond to instructions and signals in established routines, and follow relevant rules and codes.'
To these must be added:
● Children should be helped to perform movement safely, for example resilient landings.
● All equipment should be checked and well maintained.
● Teachers need to be aware of any long standing or temporary medical conditions which may restrict or inhibit participation.
● Tasks and activities will need to be modified to suit the needs of a particular group or class.
● Everyone should be aware of the safety and first-aid procedures within school.

Whatever the situation or the activity, children should be able to learn how to move under all sorts of conditions with confidence and self-control, beginning to take care of themselves and becoming aware of their responsibilities towards others. When they are using equipment, help children to be aware of the space and other people.

Planning: phases of a lesson

In school, there are, of necessity, many constraints on the ways in which we can encourage children to be physically active. Often, class size, the space and resources available prevent an individualised approach, so the lessons in this book are set out to follow a common pattern.

Preparatory activities

These include all aspects of planning that involve the children.
● Classroom preparation, for example what to wear and changing routines; discussion of safety codes; organisation of groups; reminders about responsibility for apparatus and how this will be organised; discussion of intentions or related ideas.
● Physical preparation, for example activities that will warm up the body. These need to be purposeful and clearly related to the activities that are to follow.
● General preparation, for example response activities and use of space, listening and responding.

Development

Ideas and activities are then developed in a number of ways designed to engage children in many processes of learning and much physical activity. Through a variety of movement experiences, children can be helped to explore the wide range of possibilities and increase their movement vocabulary. Structured and focused tasks and activities will help to clarify ideas and actions and the main focus will be on helping children to think, understand and make judgements.

Climax

The process of practising, consolidating, selecting and/or combining actions will involve children in choosing, performing or sharing experiences. It may involve a sequence devised in dance, gymnastics on the floor or apparatus or a small-team game.

Conclusion

This will involve a calming or concluding activity in preparation for changing and returning to the classroom; a review, discussion or evaluation of activities, in the classroom after the activity.

Assessment

Although the sequence of progression through the stages of motor development is the same for most children, they do not progress at the same rate or an even rate, so there will be a wide range of differences in the ways children achieve various actions and movements. This is natural, as every child is unique. You will be aware that sometimes, in sheer excitement or in response to the demands of a situation, a child will use inconsistent or less advanced movements. Do not worry. Observe and enjoy the actions of each child and continue to create an atmosphere of success, fun and satisfaction.

Because of the fleeting nature of physical actions, detailed observation of a class of children constantly on the move is difficult. However, it is a good idea for you to get a general impression or overall feel for the class response. Ask yourself questions like:
● How do the children respond and listen to instructions and suggestions?
● How well do they think for themselves?
● How well do they follow others?
● How well do they combine thinking as an individual with working as part of a group?

- How well do they use the space? (Could they be encouraged to use it better?)
- Are they able to use different directions?
- Are they aware of other people when they use different directions?
- How well do they sustain energetic activity?

Continual review, with a focus on a few children at a time, is recommended. Try to watch how individual children respond and move. There will be times when you note achievement that is particularly significant and times when you look for specific responses. For example:

- Do they use the whole of the body when required? Which parts could they make more use of?
- How controlled are their movements? In which ways could they refine their movements?
- Can they observe, talk about and discuss their movements and ideas and those of others?

Dance

- How well do they respond to your voice, the rhythm, sounds or music?
- How imaginative and creative are they?
- Are they achieving the qualities required? When? If not, why not? What might help?
- How well do they use individual body parts? Do they use some parts more fully than others?
- Do they use different levels of their own volition?

Gymnastics

- How do they use and handle the apparatus? Imaginatively? Responsibly?
- How inventive are their actions?
- Can they clarify and hold their shapes in balance?
- Can they take their weight confidently on their hands?
- Can they select appropriate actions that answer the task set?
- Can they link movements smoothly and imaginatively?

Games

- How confidently and agilely do they move about the space?
- How well do they stop, change direction, mark and dodge?
- How competently and confidently do they handle different pieces of equipment?
- Can they use skills, strategies and tactics to outwit an opponent?

At all times care should be taken to stress the positive aspects of the child's movement and to enjoy and encourage their attempts. There will be as many different responses as there are children and effort and progress should be acknowledged.

Differentiation

For most activities, differentiation will be *by outcome*. Tasks and problems are set which the children explore, investigate, try out, solve in different ways or are creative with, whatever their level of ability. Movement tasks and questions are open for individual interpretation, but limited enough for there to be a clear focus for attention.

Most tasks can also be *individualised*. Individual challenges can be suggested by you or made by the children. Additional support can be given, or modifications made, for individuals during the course of each lesson as you circulate and support, encourage, insist or challenge.

Sometimes there will be differentiation *by input* as you target particular children with special grouping, with suggestions (for example to make the task easier, to make it more difficult or challenging, to add an extra dimension) and with questions that vary in complexity or quality.

Dance

Dance, like language, is present in all cultures, and this chapter contains suggestions that will enable children to develop and express their ideas in movement. Emphasis is placed on encouraging children to move with confidence, often starting with actions that are familiar and that all the children can do, then developing the imaginative, creative and expressive aspects of each activity. Most children love to move to music and will gradually become more aware of and able to respond to the rhythmic qualities of dance. The appreciation and use of sounds, music and rhythms is an integral part of this process. With varied stimuli and the use of contrasting experiences, children can be helped to clarify and refine their ideas and actions, keeping in time with the accompaniment. As they develop greater control and sensitivity in their actions, they will become more aware of themselves and others and of the communicative nature of dance.

The warm-up and development aspects include listening and responding to the beat, using individual parts of the body to develop body awareness as well as warming up the body and stretching. Situations are then suggested to provide a framework for children's ideas and movements. Highlighting contrasting qualities will help children to raise their awareness of movement and clarify their actions. Through using a variety of contexts and words such as *shuffle* and *saunter* to evoke particular qualities in their actions, children will begin to understand words through their actions and refine their actions through the use of words. Within a clear framework suggested by each topic they will need time to explore and practise ideas to develop their creativity, to express themselves and sense the satisfaction from the composition of their own unique movement phrases.

It is this process of exploring, creating then linking actions which is most important, and although there are many opportunities to share and observe each other's ideas, performing to the rest of the group is not always necessary at every draft stage. Describing and discussing what they and others have done will help to develop their ability to appreciate and improve the quality of their work, but the main emphasis must be on practical participation and involvement. Some music has been suggested but percussion, or the use of sounds or words themselves will often be more readily available, simpler and a more immediate way to support children with their dance movements.

The topics for this chapter have been chosen to provide examples of using a history topic, a story and a poem as starting points for dance. Using these different stimuli will encourage children to respond in ways that challenge them physically, imaginatively and intellectually. There are opportunities to help them learn new steps, develop their responses and actions into dance-like phrases and work with others to create formations and patterns and to tell a story, thus helping to expand and enrich their experiences.

Dances from history

This unit aims to exemplify the programme of study that requires children to be taught to create and perform dances using a range of movement patterns, including those from earlier times. Learning steps and improvising, developing their ideas and planning formations, with partners or in groups, in different styles will help children to learn about dancing from different times in history.

Oliver Twist

The use of extracts from the story *Oliver Twist* by Charles Dickens as stimuli for dance provides rich opportunities for links with literacy. It will enable children to explore and respond in movement to three of the main characters in the story and help them to refine their movements. The use of the poem 'The End of the Road' by Hilaire Belloc and a variety of words for walking will help children to clarify their actions and select appropriate words for their creative writing.

Dances from history

The focus for this series of lessons will help children to understand and learn something of the different styles of dance from different periods in history.

The main emphasis is on the pavan, a slow, solemn, sedate dance said to have originated in Spain or Italy that was popular in Elizabethan times. A history topic about the Tudors might be a good starting point for this series of lessons. By researching and discussing life, entertainment and pastimes at court in Elizabethan times and musical instruments of the time, the children will find out something about the types of dances that were performed at court and those that were danced in the country.

This unit will also help to raise children's awareness of the following contrasting dances:

● the polka, popular in the 19th century

● the farandole – a dance from medieval times, performed in a line, with the leader creating various pathways and patterns, for example a spiral or snail; it was often danced on the village green at times of festivities

● the jig (sometimes spelt *gigue*) which was a popular, lively dance, usually performed on the village green

● the twist – a simple dance based on hip rotation, made famous by Chubby Checker in the early 1960s

● the charleston – an energetic dance of the 1920s with light, speedy kicks and side-steps.

The unit is divided into six sessions, allowing 30–40 minutes of activity per session. The children will create, perform and appreciate dances individually, in pairs, in groups and as a whole class.

UNIT: Dances from history

Enquiry questions	Learning objectives	Teaching activities	Learning outcomes
What are the polka and the pavan?	● Develop an awareness of space and others while dancing. ● Introduce the polka by using a side-stepping action. ● Introduce the single and double pavan step, individually and with a partner. ● Create a simple pavan dance in twos. ● Respond to two contrasting musical rhythms.	Warm-up: clapping then side-stepping to polka music, using both directions and curving pathways; trying four steps in one direction and four in another using a zigzag pathway; trying with a partner taking it in turns to lead. Development: trying slow, sedate steps to pavan music; trying the single pavan step in different directions; linking steps together to make a pattern; trying the double step. Dance: trying double then single steps with a partner using different directions; creating a pair sequence. Cool-down: individually practising a bow to greet or honour a partner.	Children: ● use the space well ● respond appropriately to different types of music
Can we improve our steps for the pavan?	● Practise and refine the polka step individually and in pairs. ● Practise and improve pavan steps individually and in pairs. ● Practise using different directions and formations. ● Create a simple pavan dance in fours.	Warm-up: tapping feet and clapping alternately changing every four beats; practising side-stepping using curving pathways; practising with a partner. Development: practising slow, sedate pavan steps; practising the single step in different directions; practising the double step; practising with a partner; trying different formations. Dance: in pairs trying different ways of turning and practising two variations; creating a sequence in pairs that includes a step pattern and some turning; in groups of four trying the double step in simple procession. Cool-down: practising a curtsy to greet or a honour partner.	● refine dance steps and keep in time with music
What is the jig? Can we perform the pavan in groups?	● Introduce the jig. ● Practise and refine the pavan step individually, in pairs and in groups. ● Practise dancing in different formations. ● Create a simple pavan dance in twos and fours.	Warm-up: practising the polka individually and then in pairs; trying a traditional hold; moving to the rhythm of the jig, clapping then slip-stepping with a bouncy step. Development: practising the slow, single and double pavan step with a partner, keeping in time with the music and each other; practising a pattern of single and double steps with a partner; deciding on starting position and clarifying the direction of movement; refining ways of turning with a partner; practising pair sequence and creating a formation. Dance: trying different ways of stepping in groups of four; practising different ways of turning in fours; creating and developing a group dance in fours, or a class dance; honouring a partner at the beginning and/or end; refining and performing. Cool-down: practising the bow and curtsy in pairs.	● work well together as a group to practise and create a dance ● use different formations

UNIT: Dances from history

Enquiry questions	Learning objectives	Teaching activities	Learning outcomes
What are the farandole and the charleston?	● Introduce the farandole. ● Respond sensitively to others in the group. ● Introduce a basic charleston rhythm and steps.	Warm-up: walking lightly individually, in pairs, fours then lines; making interesting pathways; trying the farandole and changing the leader. Development: listening to charleston music, tapping toes and stepping in time; practising a continuous rhythm of steps, getting faster and using the music; creating a pattern of tapping steps and adding a travelling step. Dance: choosing, combining and practising a step sequence on the spot, then matching a partner. Cool-down: practising a slow pavan step in pairs; stretching and relaxing.	● keep in time with the rhythm of the music
Can we improve our steps for the farandole and the charleston?	● Practise the farandole, introducing the 'snail' and 'threading the needle'. ● Practise and develop a sequence of charleston steps. ● Appreciate the work of others.	Warm-up: practising light walking step individually and in lines; trying the 'snail' (a spiral); trying 'threading the needle'. Development: practising charleston steps; trying the step turning heels out; practising a kick step; practising steps and creating a pattern of steps individually then with a partner. Dance: planning and practising a charleston dance in pairs; observing another sequence and suggesting ideas for improvement. Cool-down: practising the pavan; stretching and relaxing.	● respond to and use different forms of music ● appreciate the work of others
What is the twist? Can we perform a selection of dances?	● Introduce the twist. ● Practise and perform a selection of dances from different times in history. ● Appreciate and comment on the dances of others.	Warm-up: practising the farandole in lines, changing the leader and using different pathways. Development: trying the twist and exploring different ways of moving to music; pivoting, moving sideways and changing levels; trying this with a partner. Dance: selecting dances for everyone to perform, or groups choosing one dance, or allocating a dance to each group; practising and refining; watching half the class perform then changing over. Cool-down: practising a slow pavan step in pairs; stretching and relaxing.	● remember, practise, refine and perform chosen dances.

Cross-curricular links

History: understanding that in Elizabethan times there were no films, television, or CD players, so everyone had to make their own entertainment. Sometimes they would dance, sometimes sing or make music and sometimes act plays. As a contrast to this slow sedate dance from the 16th century, a selection can be chosen to represent different dance styles from other times in history. The farandole is an old dance from the 12th century, the jig was an improvised dance popular in the 16th and 17th centuries, and the charleston and the twist are from the 20th century.

Music: listening and responding to contrasting styles of music; keeping in time and to the rhythm of music.

Resources

A tape or CD player with selected music (for example *Firebell Polka* by Johann Strauss, 'Greensleeves', 'Let's Twist Again' by Chubby Checker); a variety of historical books for the relevant periods; photographs, pictures, artefacts, costumes or a video of the different dance styles would be useful (for example *Shakespeare in Love*); photocopiable page 128.

Display

Pictures of dancers from history; an enlarged copy of photocopiable page 128.

(35 mins) What are the polka and the pavan?

What you need and preparation

You will need a CD or tape player; polka music (such as *Firebell Polka* by Johann Strauss) and pavan music.

An extract from the video of *Shakespeare in Love* (particularly the court dance scene) might give the class a visual understanding of the costume, the dance formations and the elegance of court dances. This and further background on life and entertainment in Tudor times would be ideal starting points for this lesson.

Discuss with the children the special arrangements for changing, with reminders about getting to the hall and doing PE. Ask the class to think about the costumes the Elizabethans wore, particularly in the courts – see photocopiable page 128.

What to do

(8 mins) Warm-up

Ensure the children are in a space and start by asking them to clap in time to the polka music, for example *Firebell Polka*.

Ask them to side-step around the hall looking for spaces. Encourage use of both directions and gentle curving pathways so that good use is made of the hall space. Encourage the children to move lightly with the rhythm and use the signal *Change* to prompt them to alter direction or to use the space well. Suggest four steps in one direction and four in another with a roughly zigzag pathway. This will depend on how well the children use the space available.

Emphasise poise (keeping their heads up) and an upright stance, stretching their legs and toes. Help the children to develop an awareness of other people around them by encouraging smaller steps or steps on the spot to avoid collisions.

Ask the children to find partners and, holding fingertips lightly at arm's length, try four side-steps in one direction and four in another, changing direction alternately. Instruct the children taking the lead to steer their partners into spaces. Ensure the children take it in turns to lead.

(12 mins) Development

Remind the children of the costumes the Elizabethans wore, and ask them to show you an upright, elegant posture.

Emphasising this in their dancing, ask them, on their own, to try very slow, sedate steps to the pavan music. Encourage them to try several ways, for example lifting their knees to exaggerate slow steps; keeping their legs straight to slide their feet along the ground.

Teach them the following single pavan steps individually, starting with four slow beats. With feet together:

1. rise on toes
2. step forward on left foot
3. step forward on right foot
4. lower heels.

Practise this several times without, then with, the music. Then ask the children to try it with the other foot leading.

Help the class to practise the steps in another direction – to the left, to the right or backwards. Encourage graceful, gliding movements and solemn actions.

Ask the children to link several steps together using different directions, for example two steps forward, two steps back, two steps to the side, two steps back to the starting position or four steps forward, one to the side (right), one to the side (left).

Then teach them the double step:
1. rise on toes, start with left foot;
2. step 1, 2, 3, close, lower;
3. rise, right 2, 3, close, lower
and so on.

12 mins Dance

In pairs, ask the children to try the double step moving forward, side by side with their partners. Then ask them to try the single step, moving forward using the same leg to start as their partners.

Encourage them to try other ways of stepping together (such as away from then towards each other; sideways apart then together, forward then back, using the single or double step). Emphasise slow, sedate steps.

Play the music, asking the children to listen carefully and create a sequence in their pairs. Practise and review the sequences to finish.

Diagram 1

3 mins Cool-down

Ask the children to practise on their own the bow to greet or honour their partners. Help them with these instructions: *Standing feet slightly apart, step back on your left leg and bend the knee, keeping your right leg fairly straight; rise and close your feet.* Encourage a whole-body action. This could be done by imagining a big sweep of a hat. (See Diagram 1.) Practise together and repeat, stepping back onto the other foot, sweeping the other arm across.

Classroom review

Encourage the children to discuss and plan with their partners ways of moving to create a sequence in pairs. Ask them to think about the formation and the number of steps.

Assessing learning outcomes

Are the children able to use the space well? Are they responding appropriately to the different types of music?

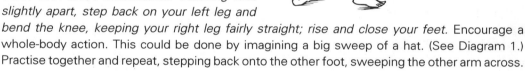

35 mins Can we improve our steps for the pavan?

What you need and preparation

You will need: a CD or cassette player; pavan music; polka music, for example *Firebell Polka*.

Recap with the children the key qualities of the polka and the pavan, and the special arrangements for changing, getting to the hall and doing PE.

What to do

8 mins Warm-up

Start by asking the children to tap one foot and then the other foot in time to the polka music (*Firebell Polka*). Then encourage them to tap their feet and clap alternately, changing every four beats.

Ask them to practise side-stepping around the hall, using gentle, curving pathways and making good use of the space. Encourage the children to change direction on the count of four beats (four in one direction, four in another – if some are finding it difficult, stick to eight). Encourage stretched legs and toes, an upright poise and an awareness of space.

Ask the children to practise this with their partners (four side-steps and change direction, with one child from each pair taking the lead to steer his or her partner into spaces around the hall). Ensure that the children take it in turns to be the leader. For those who can do this well, encourage them to change direction every two steps.

(12 mins) Development

Ask the children to practise on their own very slow, sedate steps to the music. Remind them to stand tall and to keep an elegant, upright posture.

Let them practise single steps to four slow beats, starting with feet together:

1. rise on toes
2. left foot forward
3. right foot forward
4. lower heels.

Ask the children to try this again with the other foot leading. Then encourage them to practise steps in other directions – to the left, to the right, backwards, diagonally. Remind them of the upright stance and graceful, gliding movements.

Tell the children to practise the double step (see page 14). Encourage them to listen carefully and to keep in time with the music.

Now with partners, standing side by side, ask them to practise single steps (then double steps) forward, using the same lead leg as their partners.

Encourage the pairs to try other ways of stepping together, such as away from and towards each other, sideways apart and together, forward and back, and begin to link steps together.

(12 mins) Dance

In pairs, ask the children to try different ways of slowly turning with their partner. Encourage them to try several possibilities and then practise two variations. (For example, hands held at shoulder height or take it in turns to step around their partners.) Ask them to try turning in both directions, and emphasise smooth, graceful transitions.

Ask them to create a sequence in pairs that includes a step pattern and some turning.

Organise the pairs into groups of four and tell them to try out the double step in simple procession with two following two, using a single or double step.

(3 mins) Cool-down

In twos, ask the children to practise the curtsy to greet or honour their partner. Standing with their heels together, toes turned out, encourage a slow, slight bend of the knees and rise. Ask them to try other variations of greeting or honouring their partners, for example stepping forwards, backwards or sideways into the movement.

Classroom review

Ask the children to discuss their performances and begin to record group formations in fours.

Assessing learning outcomes

Are the children able to refine the steps and keep in time with the music?

Learning objectives
- Practise and refine the polka step individually and in pairs.
- Improve the pavan step individually and in pairs.
- Practise using different directions and formations.
- Create a simple pavan dance in fours.

Lesson organisation
Recap in the classroom; warm-up individually and in pairs; development and dance individually, in pairs and fours; cool-down in pairs; teacher-led classroom review in fours.

Vocabulary
polka
pavan
procession
elegant
graceful

CHAPTER I
D·ANCE

Dances from history

35 mins What is the jig? Can we perform the pavan in groups?

Learning objectives
● Introduce the jig.
● Practise and refine pavan step individually, in pairs and in groups.
● Practise dancing in different formations.
● Create a simple pavan dance in twos and fours.

Lesson organisation
Brief classroom discussion; warm-up, development and dance individually and in pairs; paired cool-down; teacher-led classroom review.

Vocabulary
jig
polka
pavan

What you need and preparation
Organise music suitable for a pavan, jig and polka, and playback equipment.

Remind the children of the arrangements for changing, getting to the hall and doing PE. Give the children some background on the jig, explaining that it was a popular, lively dance that was usually performed on the village green.

What to do

8 mins Warm-up
Ask the children to practise the polka individually and then in pairs. Ensure that they use the space well. This could be developed by encouraging them to change direction every two steps, with a more traditional hold.

Alternatively, movement to the rhythm of a jig can be practised individually. Start by getting the whole class to clap in time to the jig music. Then ask them to slip-step around the hall with a lively, bouncy step (use a 'rumpety-tumpety' sound for the accompaniment). Encourage curving pathways so that good use is made of the hall space. Emphasise to the children that they should be lifting their knees in a light, bouncy step.

12 mins Development
In pairs, ask the children to practise the slow, single pavan step with their partners, encouraging the elegant posture they have practised. Remind them to listen carefully and keep time with each other and the music.

Go on to ask them to practise the double step, side by side with their partners (see page 14). Again, encourage the pairs to keep time with the music and each other.

Ask them to remember some of their ideas from last week and to make a pattern of single and double steps with their partners. For example, two double steps forward and two single steps sideways away from their partners, then two back together again, and repeat. Remind them to decide on starting positions and to clarify the direction of movement. Practise this together several times with the music.

Now encourage the children to think of (or remember), practise and refine some different ways of turning with their partners, using a slow, sedate step.

Ask the children to practise their pair sequence, including two different directions to create their formation, chosen from:
● away from and towards each other
● following one after the other
● together side by side
● moving apart and together, forward and back and so on.

12 mins Dance
In pairs within groups of four, ask the children to try different ways of moving together, for example facing their partners moving forward and back, then forwards and back to meet one of the other couples. (See Diagram 2 for some examples.)

Diagram 2

Now ask the children to practise different ways of turning in fours, for example all holding hands and walking in a circle, or in a star with right or left hands joining in the centre.

Help the children to go on to create and develop a group dance in fours, or even a whole-class dance. This could involve all the children in procession to start or finish. Ask them to try to add some variations to the processional dance. This could be could be rise, six steps forward close lower, rise three steps back, lower. It could also be tried moving diagonally.

Encourage the children to add honouring their partner at the beginning or end (or both). Observe and praise them as they refine and perform their dances.

(3 mins) Cool-down
Ask the children, in pairs, to practise the bow and then the curtsy to greet or honour their partners, both trying each action in turn.

Classroom review
Ask the children which formations they included in their groups of four. Encourage them to share their ideas with another group.

Assessing learning outcomes
Do the children work well together as a group to practise and create their dance? Are they using different formations?

(35 mins) What are the farandole and the charleston?

What you need and preparation
You will need: a CD or tape player; pavan music; 'Greensleeves' or 'Summer is Icumen' (on a recorder or piano); charleston music; a recorder; a drum.

Introduce the farandole to the children, explaining that it is a simple line dance.

What to do
(8 mins) Warm-up
Individually, ask the children to practise a light, happy, walking step to the sound of a recorder or light, steady drum beat. Encourage them to practise this step in pairs, then in fours, then in lines of six to eight. Ask them to try making an interesting pathway or curving pattern as they walk, emphasising leading around other lines.

Introduce the farandole and teach the children to change the leader in the following way: the first two dancers make an arch, and the others walk through, one of whom becomes the new leader; the first dancers then join the end of the line (like 'Oranges and lemons' – see Diagram 3).

(14 mins) Development
Introduce the charleston music and ask the children to tap their toes in time with it. Encourage them to use both feet, in turn, then ask them to try out some different steps.

Teach tap in front with left foot and then back together, then tap in front with right foot and then back together. Practise a continuous rhythm of steps, gradually getting faster to try it with the music.

Diagram 3

**Lesson
organisation**
Classroom
introduction;
warm-up and
practice
individually and in
pairs and groups;
paired cool-down;
teacher-led
classroom review.

Encourage the children to try the tap in other directions, for example point and tap with left foot to the left and then back together; tap behind with right foot and then back together.

Ask them to create a pattern of tapping steps, for example two to the left, two to the right; or one to the front, one to the left, one to the front, one to the right.

Then ask them to try to add a travelling step, such as step forward onto the left foot and tap forward with the right foot; step back on the right foot and tap back with the left foot. Encourage crisp, precise steps.

(9 mins) Dance

Ask the children to choose, combine and practise to compose a pattern or sequence of charleston steps on the spot, individually and then matching a partner.

(4 mins) Cool-down

In pairs, ask the children to practise one of the slow pavan steps. Invite everyone to stretch and relax to finish.

Classroom review

Ask the children if they enjoyed the charleston. *What did you like about it?*

Vocabulary
charleston
farandole

Assessing learning outcomes

Can the children keep in time with the rhythm of the music?

(35 mins) Can we improve our steps for the farandole and the charleston?

**Learning
objectives**
● Practise the
farandole,
introducing the
'snail' and
'threading the
needle'.
● Practise and
develop a sequence
of charleston steps.
● Appreciate the
work of others.

**Lesson
organisation**
Brief classroom
discussion; warm-
up individually and
in lines; practise of
the charleston
individually and in
pairs; cool-down in
fours; classroom
review in pairs.

What you need and preparation

You will need a CD or tape player; music for the pavan, charleston and farandole.

Before moving to the hall, remind the children of dances they have practised and introduce the twist.

What to do

Diagram 4

(8 mins) Warm-up

Ask the children to practise the light, happy, walking step, individually and then in lines of six to eight. Practise with the first pair making an arch on your signal for the others to step through. Practise this several times so that everyone has an opportunity to be a leader.

Introduce the 'snail'. Explain that the leader takes the line into a spiral (like a snail shell). Once in the spiral, everyone pauses and walks on the spot. Ask the leader, then everyone in the line, to turn around. The end person becomes the new leader to lead the line into a new space. (See Diagram 4.)

Introduce 'threading the needle'. The first dancer leads the line through the arches made by the raised hands of the other dancers. Try this at first when the line is still.

Vocabulary
farandole
spiral
snail
threading the
    needle

12 **Development**
mins Ask the children to practise some of the charleston steps they tried last week. Then teach them to march lightly on the spot, then turn their heels out to the side (see Diagram 5). Try this with charleston music.

Tell the children to practise stepping onto their left foot and kicking forward with the right and vice versa. Encourage them to develop a kicking action to kick across the body (see Diagram 6), for example: *Step forward on your right foot and kick your left foot across to the right.*

Ask everyone to practise their favourite charleston steps and create a pattern of steps.

Then ask them to try matching their steps to those of a partner. Invite them to add some more ideas of their own if they can. They could try this side by side or facing each other with one person moving forward and the other backward.

Diagram 5

Diagram 6

11 **Dance**
mins Thinking of these formations, ask all the children, in their pairs, to plan and practise a charleston dance.

Then ask each pair to observe another pair's sequence and comment on one positive aspect (something they particularly liked or thought was done well). Encourage them also to suggest some ideas for improvement. Tell everyone to repeat their dances, taking into account any suggestions made.

4 **Cool-down**
mins Ask the children to practise the pavan procession in fours. Finish by telling everyone to stretch and relax.

Classroom review
With their partner, ask the children to describe their charleston dance.

Assessing learning outcomes
Are the children responding to and using the different forms of music? Are they able to appreciate the work of others?

40 mins What is the twist? Can we perform a selection of dances ?

Learning objectives
● Introduce the twist.
● Practise and perform a selection of dances from different times in history.
● Appreciate and comment on the dances of others.

Lesson organisation
Classroom discussion; warm-up in lines, practise the twist individually and in pairs; choice of dance in groups; cool-down in pairs; teacher-led classroom review.

Vocabulary
twist
gyrate
levels
high
medium
low

What you need and preparation
You will need a CD or cassette player; music for the charleston, farandole, twist (for example 'Let's Twist Again' by Chubby Checker), pavan and polka.

Before going to the hall, explain to the children that the focus for this lesson is on selecting favourite dances in groups.

What to do

5 mins Warm-up
Ask the children to practise the farandole in lines of six to eight.
Remind them how to practise changing the leader, making an arch and different pathways.

10 mins Development
Introduce the music of the twist and ask the children if they have seen this dance performed or know how to do it. Ask them to try different ways of moving to the music.

Then teach them to pivot on the balls of their feet. Ask them to slowly twist (gyrate) their hips from side to side, pivoting on the spot. Gradually speed up the twisting action in time with the music ('Let's Twist Again').

Ask them to try the following:
● twist and travel – feet pivoting and gradually moving sideways
● twist and change levels, keep moving from low to high to low and so on
● with a partner, one leading and the other following the action
● with a partner, using different levels – when one goes high the other sinks low (see Diagram 7).

Diagram 7

20 mins Dance
Either select one (or two) of the dances for everyone to perform, or ask the groups to choose one of the dances, or allocate one dance to each group. Give them time to practise and refine the dance, developing and clarifying the ideas they have developed over the past few weeks, and deciding on starting and finishing positions and formations.

If appropriate, half the groups can watch the other half and then change over.
If there is time, choose another dance for the groups to practise and then perform.

5 mins Cool-down
In pairs, ask the children to practise one of the slow pavan steps. Ask them to stretch and relax to finish.

Classroom review
Which of the dances did the children enjoy most and why? Ask them to describe what they liked about the dances performed. *What were the differences between them?*

Assessing learning outcomes
Can the children remember, practise, refine and perform the dances chosen?

Follow-up activity
A similar line dance to the farandole is danced in Greece, based on the legend of the labyrinth. Try using music like the theme from *Zorba the Greek* and make up a step pattern.

Oliver Twist

This unit uses an extract from *Oliver Twist* by Charles Dickens as a stimulus for dance. Children will be able to explore individually and in groups and respond in movement to some of the characters in the story to create a simple dance narrative. They will be encouraged to use their imaginations, clarify and refine their actions appropriate to the characters and select and sequence their actions in time with an accompaniment.

This unit will use an extract from chapters 8–10 of *Oliver Twist*. The following dramatic ideas from these chapters of the story will be used as a basis for the dance:

● Fagin examining the treasures.
● Oliver waking up and dressing.
● Creeping, dodging and stopping.
● Following the Artful Dodger.
● Bumping into Mr Brownlow at the bookshop – caught?

Using the framework of the extract will help children to identify and select aspects of the story (for example Fagin's den), and will provide the opportunity to explore the actions of travelling, turning, gesture and stillness, and to consider contrasts in shape, level, speed and direction.

Because one of the key movement themes is moving and stopping, children will need to listen and practise responding to a musical accompaniment and to their partners, using different roles (leading and following; advancing and retreating).

Children will be able to explore the movement and moods of the selected characters and develop and practise their ideas to portray the three key characters in this extract to represent:

● an old, shrivelled, miserly man – Fagin
● a frightened, innocent young boy – Oliver
● a swaggering young man – the Artful Dodger.

This will encourage them to explore and develop gesturing movements, the space around their body and pauses with held body shapes (wide, narrow, curled and twisted). All the children will be able to experience the movements of each of the different characters individually and then collaborate with a group to combine and link phrases of movement to develop a performance.

A focus on the use of different words for walking using the poem 'The End of the Road' by Hilaire Belloc (provided on photocopiable page 129) will help the children develop both their word and movement vocabulary and refine ways of travelling. Use of contrasting words for walking in each lesson, some of which they will use in their dance, will help children to select and highlight the significant qualities, clarify their actions and develop dance phrases.

The poem can be used at the beginning or at any point during the unit to highlight the different words for walking. It will help in encouraging children to think of as many different words as they can to describe walking actions: trudge, strut, stroll, swagger, amble, hobble, stride, saunter, limp and so on.

This unit is divided into six sessions, allowing 30–45 minutes of activity per session. The children will create, perform, think about and appreciate dances individually, in pairs, in groups or as a whole class.

UNIT: Oliver Twist

Enquiry questions	Learning objectives	Teaching activities	Learning outcomes
How might Fagin move?	• Practise moving and stopping in time with an accompaniment. • Explore and practise different words for walking – *march* and *hobble*. • Explore and represent the character of Fagin in phrases of movement. • Practise and refine miserly gestures.	Warm-up: listening, clapping and marching to the music; striding in different ways and directions and freezing the action (like 'Musical statues'); following a partner marching. Development: practising contrasting walking action; trying hobbling; practising key qualities; linking together aspects of hobbling; selecting words, still shapes and actions to represent Fagin; thinking how Fagin might look at the jewellery; listening and matching movements with the music; exaggerating the actions and developing a phrase to the music; trying sweeping an arm into a turn. Dance: listening to the music and planning starting position as Fagin; choosing actions to link together. Cool-down: stepping slowly; swaying gently from side to side, then relaxing.	Children: • represent Fagin's miserly character • extend mimed actions into dance-like phrases • demonstrate marching and hobbling qualities
How might Oliver move?	• Practise and improve moving and stopping in time with an accompaniment. • Explore and practise different words for walking – *striding*, *creeping* and *shuffling*. • Practise and refine actions by focusing on individual body parts, levels and directions. • Explore and develop the character of Oliver – frightened young boy. • Practise stretching and reaching in different directions using different levels. • Represent Oliver waking and dressing in movement.	Warm-up: striding purposefully to the beat, swinging arms and using straight pathways; shaking knees and other parts of the body. Development: practising quiet, timid, stealthy qualities in creeping actions; developing a creeping phrase; refining the qualities; linking three different ways of creeping and pausing; practising shuffling their feet; adding a shuffling step to Fagin's character; choosing shapes to represent a frightened Oliver; practising cowering and turning and crouching; adding a shaking action; practising drowsy and yawning actions, reaching and stretching in different directions. Dance: starting in sleeping posture; sleepily stretching and yawning; practising Fagin examining the treasures; in pairs practising Fagin examining the treasures and Oliver waking up. Cool-down: swaying to the music; drawing a big figure of eight shape in the air smoothly; practising with a partner; relaxing.	• listen and respond in time with music • refine a creeping action • represent the characters of Oliver and Fagin
How might the Artful Dodger move?	• Explore and practise different words for walking – *stamping* and *dodging*. • Develop a creeping sequence in twos, leading and following. • Practise creeping and stopping using different body shapes	Warm-up: walking, then jogging, weaving in and out of a small space; dodging in and out, changing direction and stopping suddenly; clapping and stamping their feet; stamping a rhythm for a partner to echo; circling their hips, changing direction; moving their elbows together and apart. Development: practising the swaggering action of the Artful Dodger, then dodging, shadowing their partner's movements; refining the action thinking about body posture; strolling and pausing to look; following a partner dodging or crouching down to hide; planning and practising a phrase with a partner. Dance: practising dodging and following and hiding actions. Cool-down: swaying and drawing shapes in the air; trying ideas for a cool-down sequence in pairs; relaxing.	• demonstrate the different qualities required as they creep, dodge and stamp • use different directions and levels • make different shapes for hiding positions

Enquiry questions	Learning objectives	Teaching activities	Learning outcomes
Can we stroll, swagger, dodge and creep?	● Explore and practise different words for walking – *dashing*, *strolling* and *staggering*. ● Practise dodging and hiding to the music. ● Start to create a cool-down sequence in pairs.	Warm-up: walking in different directions; practising strolling or sauntering, emphasising curving pathways; circling shoulders; shaking feet. Development: dashing to and fro; limping and swaggering; describing and practising a following, dodging phrase; practising with a partner, one walking, one dodging and creeping. Dance: listening and practising with the music, distinguishing between steps of the Dodger and the frightened steps and shaking of Oliver; practising part of the dance and evaluating. Cool-down: making up and combining ideas for a cool-down sequence with a partner, matching or mirroring, leading and following; relaxing.	● start to compose a cool-down sequence ● working well together ● demonstrate dashing, strolling and swaggering qualities
Can we refine our dance actions and phrases?	● Explore and practise different words for walking – *strutting* and *ambling*. ● Represent the frightened Oliver following the Artful Dodger in phrases of movement. ● Combine the different aspects of the story in movement.	Warm-up: strolling, using different directions; developing stroll, pause, stroll, turn; striding; moving parts of the body to the beat. Development: beckoning large and small actions; shivering and shaking; combining creeping and shaking; creeping and following; following and walking stealthily. Dance: practising phrases of movement in pairs, matching silence and stillness and movement and sound; choosing and practising other parts of the dance; discussing and reviewing. Cool-down: practising cool-down sequence with a partner; relaxing.	● refine their movements ● respond well to music
Can we perform an extract from *Oliver Twist* in dance?	● Practise, combine, refine and perform an extract from *Oliver Twist*. ● Evaluate own and others' performances. ● Create and refine characters in dance.	Warm-up: choosing and practising one way of walking; making shapes then stopping in character; creeping and matching actions to the music; choosing two actions, moving parts of the body and practising with the accompaniment. Development: practising the opening sequence with Oliver sleeping and Fagin examining his treasures; practising dodging and following in Fagin's den and following the Artful Dodger to the bookshop. Dance: discussing the ending of the dance – the Artful Dodger bumping into Mr Brownlow – timing movement to the music, the Artful Dodger running and hiding and Oliver caught. Cool-down: in pairs, performing the cool-down sequence.	● remember and perform a dance in groups.

Cross-curricular links
English: using verbs – past, present and future tenses; expanding vocabulary to enhance creative writing; looking at Charles Dickens's *Oliver Twist* and 'The End of the Road' by Hilaire Belloc.
History: exploring Victorian living and working conditions, child labour and workhouses.
Music: listening and responding in movement; appreciation of phrases and phrasing.

Resources
A tape or CD player; Mussorgsky's *Pictures at an Exhibition* – 'Promenade' and 'Gnome'; Gershwin's 'Walking the Dog' or Leroy Anderson's 'Jazz Pizzicato'; the theme from *Schindler's List* or 'Skye' by John Williams; a lively march such as a Johann Strauss's 'Radetsky March' or 'The Dambusters March' by Eric Coates; photocopiable page 129.

🕐 35 mins How might Fagin move?

Learning objectives
● Practise moving and stopping in time with an accompaniment.
● Explore different words for walking – *march* and *hobble*.
● Explore and represent the character of Fagin in phrases of movement.
● Practise and refine miserly gestures.

Lesson organisation
Reading and discussion in the classroom; individual and paired warm-up; development and dance individually and in pairs; individual cool-down; teacher-led classroom review.

What you need and preparation
You will need: a CD or tape player; 'Radetsky March' by Johann Strauss or 'The Dambusters March' by Eric Coates; the theme tune from *Schindler's List* or 'Skye' both by John Williams; 'Promenade' from *Pictures at an Exhibition* by Mussorgsky; a tambour or wood block.

Discuss with the children the special arrangements for doing PE.

Read Chapter 8 of *Oliver Twist* and discuss Fagin's character and movement.

What to do

🕐 6 mins Warm-up
Starting with all the children in their own space, ask them to listen, then clap, then march on the spot to the music. Use a lively march such as 'Radetsky March'. Then tell them to stride out around the hall, moving in different directions. Encourage different variations of stride (for example high knee lifts or straight legs) and different ways of using their arms (straight by their sides, behind their backs, elbows swinging to each side). Now and then, stop the music and encourage the children to freeze the action until the music resumes (like 'Musical statues').

In pairs, ask the children to take it in turns to be leader, with their partners following and matching their marching actions. Encourage strong, purposeful movements.

Now individually, ask them to shrug their shoulders in time with the beat of the tambour or wood block. Repeat a phrase (for example up and down, up and down, up and down and stop). Similarly, practise stretching and clenching fingers in time with the same accompaniment.

🕐 14 mins Development
Ask the children to think of a word for walking that contrasts with *marching*. Ask them to think about the word *hobble* and to try that in movement. Encourage them to select the key qualities – uneven, irregular, moving from side to side, limping – and to exaggerate those in their actions. To help them to develop a dance phrase, ask them to select two aspects of the hobbling action and to link them together and repeat them (for example limp and limp in one direction and pause, limp and pause, limp and limp in another direction and pause). Encourage them to think about the body posture, the head and arm actions and to practise and refine these actions. Ask them to put more weight and emphasis on one side of the body and then to try that on the other side. With partners, encourage them to observe and help each other to refine the movements.

Ask the children to think about the character of Fagin and to choose some words that might describe him and his movements – in Dickens's words, *a very old, shrivelled Jew*. Ask them to show you a still shape to represent the character, then another and another. What about the facial expression? (*With a villainous look and repulsive face.*) How might he stand or sit? How would he move? How would an old person move? What would he be doing?

Encourage the children to use their ideas to move slowly and unevenly.

Move on to ask them to think how Fagin might look at the jewellery, pulling it out slowly from a small box from a trap door in the floor and holding the pieces up in the air to see them sparkle or assess their value (*took a magnificent, sparkling gold watch with jewels from the box and surveyed it with pleasure*). Tell the children to listen to the music (long, slow chords) and try to match movements with the music. (Count 11, for example, to lift the watch; stretch a hand in the air; hold the watch up, move it from side to side and slowly return it to the box.)

Vocabulary
stride
march
hobble
limp
irregular
exaggerate
refine
contrast
miserly
hoard
stingy
secretive
surveyed

Ask the children to be secretive in their movements, often turning their heads stiffly and slowly, bending and hiding what they have in front of them. Tell them to practise stretching and closing their hands and rubbing them together.

Ask them what Fagin might be wearing. Can they include some arm actions that enclose the body, wrapping a cloak around, and hiding what it is in his pockets? Encourage them to use alternate arms and make these actions larger than life. Ask them to develop them into a phrase to the beginning of 'Promenade'. Prompt them by asking: *Can you slowly sweep your arm around into a turn?*

12 mins Dance

Ask the children to listen to the extract from the music and to plan their starting position as Fagin. Let them choose the order of their actions, but encourage them to include some of the following:

● turning their heads stiffly and slowly, bending and hiding
● shuffling or hobbling slowly backwards and forwards
● pulling out jewellery from under the floorboards or hiding place and holding it up in the air
● stretching and closing their hands and rubbing them together
● sweeping their cloaks around to hide their treasures.

3 mins Cool-down

To the theme music from *Schindler's List*, ask the children to listen then step slowly in time with the music. Can they make big slow steps? Can they use different directions? Ask them to sway gently from side to side, transferring their weight from one foot to the other and then to relax.

Classroom review

Ask the children to describe Fagin's actions to a partner. Encourage their discussion by asking questions such as: *Which words and actions describe his character?*

Assessing learning outcomes

Are the children able to represent Fagin's miserly character? Did they extend the mimed actions into dance-like phrases? Can they demonstrate marching and hobbling qualities?

Oliver Twist

35 mins How might Oliver move?

Learning objectives
● Practise and improve moving and stopping in time with an accompaniment.
● Explore and practise different words for walking – *striding*, *creeping* and *shuffling*.
● Refine actions by focusing on individual body parts, levels and directions.
● Explore and develop the character of Oliver – a frightened young boy.
● Practise stretching and reaching in different directions using different levels.
● Represent Oliver waking and dressing in movement.

Lesson organisation
Brief classroom discussion; individual warm-up and development; dance and cool-down individually and in pairs; teacher-led classroom review.

Vocabulary
shuffle
hunched
drowsy
tempo
stride
creep
stealthily
crouching
hiding
cowering

What you need and preparation
You will need: a CD or tape player; the theme tune from *Schindler's List*; 'Promenade' from *Pictures at an Exhibition* by Mussorgsky; bells; tambour; tambourine.

Talk about what the children know already of *Oliver Twist* and discuss how frightened Oliver must have felt in Fagin's den. Remind the children of the arrangements for changing, getting to the hall and doing PE.

What to do

5 mins Warm-up
Ask the children to stride steadily and purposefully around the hall to the beat of the tambour and to change direction on a double beat. Encourage them to swing their arms, use straight pathways and to change direction sharply. Vary the speed of this action and encourage the children to respond as the tempo changes.

Tell them to shake their knees in time with the shaking tambourine, stopping each time the sound stops (shake and shake and shake and stop). Repeat a similar phrase for shaking other parts of the body (hands, shoulders, hips and so on).

Ask them to try a heel and toe action, tapping the floor in time with the tapping of the tambourine accompaniment, again listening and stopping when the sound stops.

14 mins Development
Ask the children for words to describe a creeping action, for example *quietly*, *timidly*, *stealthily*, *unobserved*, *slowly*, *quickly*, *lightly*. Discuss with them how they might show these qualities in their movements and then ask them to practise this. Encourage them to try several ways with an accompaniment (saying the words or light shaking of bells) to provide a framework for their actions. For example, creep, and creep and creep and pause. Repeat it three times.

Help the children to refine these qualities by focusing on individual parts of the body with the following questions:
● What exactly are your feet doing? Which part of your foot touches the floor?
● What do you do with your hands and your head?
● Which direction are you moving in?
● Which level – high, medium or low?
Ask them to link three different ways of creeping:
● creep and creep and creep and look (twice)
● creep and creep and creep and stop in a shape.
Encourage them to listen for the silence and to pause or freeze like a statue when the bells stop. Repeat and practise, particularly encouraging them to use different levels. Vary the speed of the accompaniment so that one phrase encourages a quicker creeping action.

Ask them to think about the word *shuffle* and to try that in movement. Encourage them to select the key qualities – dragging or sliding their feet along the ground – and to practise them.

Help the children make up a phrase – shuffle, shuffle in one direction, shuffle, shuffle in another. Ask them to think of Fagin's character and to think what they need to add to the shuffling step (such as a hunched shape and twisted hands).

Ask the children how they think Oliver must have felt in Fagin's den. *How would a frightened young boy stand or sit? If he were frightened how would he move?* Encourage them to show you a still shape to represent the character of Oliver, and another, and another. *Which way might he move?*

Introduce *cowering* and ask the children to turn and crouch, tiptoe into a new space and turn and crouch again. Repeat this, looking around and shaking different parts of the body. Emphasise withdrawing and closing the body.

Discuss being drowsy and not quite awake and then practise stretching out in a big yawn. Try this in different ways, reaching and stretching in different directions (along the floor, out to the side, upwards). Encourage the children to make the actions as large and as smooth and continuous as possible, curling and closing their bodies in between each stretch or yawn, returning to a sleeping posture after each one.

12 mins Dance
Ask the children to think of a sleeping posture for the starting position and then to try out other ways they could do this (curl up, sitting with hands in head or lie stretched out). Slowly and sleepily ask them to stretch out in a big yawn and to change their sleeping position. Repeat several times in time with the accompaniment ('Promenade' from *Pictures at an Exhibition*). Emphasise slow, continuous actions. Then ask them to practise Fagin examining the treasures to the same accompaniment.

In pairs, ask one partner to represent Fagin examining the treasures, while the other represents Oliver waking up, using the different ways they have just practised. Ensure that they take turns to try each character.

4 mins Cool-down
Play the theme from *Schindler's List* and ask the class to sway in time to the music with smooth, slow actions. Ask them to use one hand to draw a big figure of eight shape in the air. Ask them to do that with the other hand and then to try some other patterns of their own, making the shapes as big and as smooth as possible.

In pairs, ask them to step slowly towards their partners. Ask them to draw the figure of eight or their own shapes in time with the music, with their partners following. Remind them to take it in turns to lead. Then let everyone relax.

Classroom review

Ask the children to discuss how Oliver might have felt, and how they managed to represent this in movement. *How might you improve this next time?*

Assessing learning outcomes

Are the children listening and responding in time with the music? Have they refined the creeping action? Are they able to represent the characters of Oliver and Fagin?

Oliver Twist

35 mins How might the Artful Dodger move?

Learning objectives
● Explore and practise different words for walking – *stamping* and *dodging*.
● Develop a creeping sequence in twos, leading and following.
● Practise creeping and stopping using different body shapes.

Lesson organisation
Brief discussion in the classroom; individual and paired warm-up; development, dance and cool-down in pairs; teacher-led classroom review.

What you need and preparation
You will need: a CD or tape player; a drum or tambour; tambourine; 'Gnome' extract from *Pictures at an Exhibition*; the theme tune to *Schindler's List*.

Talk with the children about the use of gesture to enhance characterisation and discuss the words *swagger* and *artful. When have they practised dodging before?* Revise the special arrangements for doing PE.

What to do

6 mins Warm-up
Ask the children to walk, then jog, to the shaking tambourine, steadily weaving in and out of each other around the hall. Gradually speed up the action and reduce the space using half, then a third of the floor space. Encourage the children to freeze when the music stops and to change direction suddenly on the command *Change*. Use the word *Dodge* (as they do in games) to help them to move quickly to and fro without touching anyone else. Practise weaving in and out of each other, changing direction and stopping suddenly.

Play a strong beat on the drum or tambour, asking the children to reply, firstly clapping and then stamping their feet (bang, bang, bang – stamp, stamp, stamp). Encourage strength throughout the body but without slapping their feet on the floor. Instruct everyone to try this on the spot and then travelling. Vary the rhythm to encourage careful listening and responding to the beat.

In pairs, ask the children in turn to stamp a rhythm for their partners to echo. Practise this several times, making sure that they take it in turns to stamp a rhythm. Encourage them to match arm actions too. Emphasise repeating the phrase to create the rhythm.

Now on their own, ask the children to circle their hips in time with the shaking tambourine, stopping and changing direction each time the shaking stops. Encourage them to make the circle as big as they can.

Ask them to bring their elbows together and apart in time with the tapping of the tambourine accompaniment, again listening and stopping when the sound stops.

Oliver Twist

Development

14 mins Ask the class to think about the character of the Artful Dodger – *a swaggering, young man*. Can they remember the discussion in the classroom and what these words mean? Ask them to face their partners and for one of each pair to move from side to side to practise dodging. Ask their partners to shadow their movements. Make sure they take turns.

What else do the children think they could show in their movements about the character of the artful dodger? *How might he move?* (Confidently, casually, sauntering along.) Encourage them to think about body posture, head and arm actions, and even facial expression, and to practise and refine these actions.

Ask one of the children from each pair to walk or stroll about the space, pausing now and again to look around or into a shop window. See if their partners can follow them without being seen. Can they dodge out of the way or crouch down when their partners look? Ask them to take it in turns to be the follower. Tell the pairs to plan and practise a phrase so that they know which way they will turn (for example pause to look to the right, change direction, pause to look to the left), so that they can combine their movements.

Ask the children what shapes they could make when they are hiding. Introduce the four main body shapes for them to try and adapt:
● wide, flat shape – for example against a wall
● curled, small shape – crouching down to hide
● long, tall, thin shape – for example behind a post
● twisted shape – turn the upper part of the body and freeze as if part of them was going in the other direction.

Dance

12 mins Play the first part of 'Gnome' from *Pictures at an Exhibition* and encourage the children to work out the first four phrases with one dodging and the partner following. Relate this to the Artful Dodger teaching Oliver to dodge and hide. For the fourth phrase, encourage light, tiptoe steps, picking up the feet. Each phrase should end with a sudden stop when the position is held. Help the children to try to distinguish between the bolder steps of the Artful Dodger and the more timid steps of Oliver. Let the children practise it several times to match the movements to the music.

Cool-down

3 mins Play the theme from *Schindler's List* and ask the class to sway in time to the music with smooth, slow actions. Remind them of the shapes in the air that they made up last week with their partner and to practise those to the music. Explain that you want them to make up a cool-down sequence in pairs. Ask them to try some other ways of moving with their partners, taking it in turns to lead. For example, ask them if they can circle their arms in time with the music. Finish by asking everyone to relax.

Classroom review

Ask the children to discuss and plan some ideas for their cool-down sequence. *Can you find ways of recording your ideas so that you remember them for next time?*

Assessing learning outcomes

Can the children demonstrate the different qualities required as they creep, dodge and stamp? Are they using different directions and levels? Are they making different shapes for their hiding positions?

Oliver Twist

(35 mins) Can we stroll, swagger, dodge and creep?

Learning objectives
● Explore and practise different words for walking – *dashing*, *strolling* and *staggering*.
● Practise dodging and hiding to the music.
● Start to create a cool-down sequence in pairs.

Lesson organisation
Reading and discussion in the classroom; individual warm-up; development and dance individually and in pairs; cool-down individually; teacher-led classroom review.

Vocabulary
dashing
strolling
sauntering
limping
swaggering
dodging
hiding

What you need and preparation

You will need: a CD or tape player; Gershwin's 'Walking the Dog' or music in a similar relaxed style, for example 'Jazz Pizzicato' by Leroy Anderson; 'Gnome' from *Pictures at an Exhibition*; the theme to *Schindler's List*; a tambourine; tambour.

Discuss more words for walking, referring to the poem 'The End of the Road' by Hilaire Belloc, on photocopiable page 129. Talk about the special arrangements for changing, getting to the hall and doing PE.

What to do

(6 mins) **Warm-up**
Individually, ask the children to walk in different directions around the hall to the light tap of the tambourine. Start steadily and then gradually increase the speed until they are walking at a brisk pace.

Then ask them if they can remember a word for leisurely walking from the poem by Hilaire Belloc (*strolling, sauntering*). Ask: *What are the essential qualities?* (Casual, relaxed.) Encourage them to try to emphasise those. Suggest that they try sauntering, emphasising curving pathways, then try this using the music from 'Walking the Dog' (or the light tap of the tambour). *How might you use your arms?* (Gently swinging, loosely by their sides, for example.)

Ask the children to circle their shoulders in time with the shaking tambourine, stopping and changing direction each time the shaking stops. Encourage them to make their circles as big as they can.

Ask them to shake their feet one at a time with the shaking tambourine accompaniment, again listening and changing feet or stopping when the sound stops.

(14 mins) **Development**
Ask the children to walk briskly, dashing to and fro, then ask them to try limping and swaggering. Let them try this using the music of 'Walking the Dog'.

In pairs, ask them to describe and then practise the phrase they made up with their partner so that when one is following they know which way their partner will turn and they can dodge out of the way or hide. Each time they stop, ask them to hold a different shape to hide. Remind them of the different shapes as they do this – wide, curled, long thin or twisted.

Ask them to practise dodging, taking it in turns to shadow their partner, one walking, one creeping up behind.

(12 mins) Dance

Play the first part of 'Gnome' from *Pictures at an Exhibition* and ask the children to listen and then practise, with one of them dodging and the partner following, to the first four phrases of the music. Practise matching the movements with the music several times.

Then listen to the next phrases of 'Gnome' and practise dodging and hiding with a sudden stop and held position. Remind the children to distinguish between the bolder steps of the Artful Dodger and the even more frightened steps of Oliver. *How would you show in movement that you were very frightened? Can you exaggerate this and develop it into a phrase?* (For example, shake knees, shake whole body and cower and hide.)

Invite them to choose one section of the dance to practise, and help them to discuss and think how they might improve the actions.

(3 mins) Cool-down

Play the theme from *Schindler's List* and ask the class to try some of their ideas for their cool-down sequence with their partner, matching or mirroring, leading and following or contrasting (one high, one low). Then ask them to relax.

Classroom review

Ask the children to listen carefully to the music and to visualise and plan their actions. Encourage them to discuss these with their partners.

Assessing learning outcomes

Are the children able to start to compose a cool-down sequence? How well are they working together? Do they demonstrate dashing, strolling and swaggering qualities?

(35 mins) Can we refine our dance actions and phrases?

What you need and preparation

You will need: a CD player or tape deck; 'Gnome' and 'Promenade' from *Pictures at an Exhibition*; 'Walking the Dog'; the theme tune to *Schindler's List*; a tambour; tambourine.

Recap the parts of *Oliver Twist* read and the dances covered so far. Discuss with the children the special arrangements for changing, getting to the hall and doing PE.

What to do

(5 mins) Warm-up

Play the Gershwin music and ask the class to practise strolling, using different directions. Can they develop a phrase which they can repeat (stroll, pause, stroll, turn, stroll)?

Using a tambour, play some strong beats and encourage the children to stride purposefully around the hall. Again, ask them to develop a phrase that they can repeat (stride, stride, stride and turn, stride and turn).

Ask them to swing their hips from side to side in time with the tapping tambourine, stopping each time the sound stops.

Now ask the children to choose one of the actions, or make up a new one of their own, to practise with the shaking tambourine accompaniment, again listening out and stopping when the sound stops.

> **Learning objectives**
> ● Explore and practise different words for walking – *strutting* and *ambling*.
> ● Represent the frightened Oliver following the Artful Dodger in phrases of movement.
> ● Combine the different aspects of the story in movement.
>
> **Lesson organisation**
> Revision in the classroom; individual warm-up; development and dance in pairs; cool-down in pairs then individually; teacher-led classroom review.

Oliver Twist

(12 mins) Development

In pairs, ask the children to try different ways in which they can beckon to their partner to encourage them to follow. Encourage them to use exaggerated circling actions and quick, small, impatient actions.

Ask them how they might show in their movement how afraid Oliver is. Help them to practise the shivering and shaking actions in the knees, shoulders and hands. Encourage them by asking: *Can you combine the creeping and shaking?* Practise this to the first part of 'Gnome'.

Ask the children to practise with one person creeping and the other (representing Oliver) following. Then practise this to the second part of 'Gnome' when Oliver follows the Artful Dodger as he *walked stealthily across the road and slunk close behind the old gentleman.*

(15 mins) Dance

In pairs, ask the children to practise several times with the 'Gnome' music, trying to match the phrasing of the sound with the phrases of movement. Emphasise silence and stillness and movement and sound.

Ask them to choose and practise the other parts of the dance to 'Promenade', thinking of ways it might be refined with both partners trying each character. Discuss and review this together afterwards.

(3 mins) Cool-down

Play the theme from *Schindler's List* and ask the class to try some of their ideas for their cool-down sequence with their partners, matching or leading and following. Then finish with everyone stopping their practice and relaxing.

Classroom review

Ask the children to think about and review their actions.

Assessing learning outcomes

Are the children able to refine their movements? How well are they responding to the music?

(35 mins) Can we perform an extract from Oliver Twist in dance?

What you need and preparation

You will need: a CD or tape player; 'Promenade' and 'Gnome' from *Pictures at an Exhibition*; 'Walking the Dog'; the *Schindler's List* theme tune; a tambourine.

Discuss the special arrangements for changing, getting to the hall and doing PE.

What to do

(6 mins) Warm-up

Using the Gershwin music, ask the class to choose and then practise one of the ways of walking. Stop the music after different intervals and ask the class to make one of the following shapes – wide and narrow or curled and twisted. Then ask them to stop in the posture of one of the characters. Is it clear which one is which?

Then ask the children to practise creeping on their own, matching their actions to the music ('Gnome' from *Pictures at an Exhibition*). Encourage them to listen carefully to the phrasing.

Ask them to choose two of the actions, moving parts of the body, or make up two of their own, one with the shaking tambourine accompaniment, and one with the tapping tambourine accompaniment, stopping when the sound stops.

(12 mins) Development

In pairs, ask the children to practise the opening sequence with Oliver sleeping and Fagin examining his treasures, using 'Promenade' from *Pictures at an Exhibition*. Ask: *How could you make the action clearer? Can you use your whole body much more?*

Ask the children to practise the dodging and following sequence, trying to refine their actions in time with 'Gnome':

● Creeping, dodging and stopping in Fagin's den.
● Following the Artful Dodger towards the man at the bookshop.
  Ensure that the children take it in turns to play each character.

(14 mins) Dance

As a class, remind the children of and discuss the ending of the dance. (The Artful Dodger bumps into Mr Brownlow, the man at the bookshop.) Together, listen to the music ('Gnome') and time the clash. NB. This should not be a physical bump, but encourage large gestures. (The Artful Dodger moves away and hides and Oliver shakes in fright, turns around and is caught.)

Go on to help the children practise and perform the whole dance:

● Oliver sleeping and Fagin examining the treasures
● the creeping, dodging and following sequence in Fagin's den
● following the Artful Dodger towards the bookshop
● the clash with Mr Brownlow.

(3 mins) Cool-down

In pairs, ask the children to perform their cool-down sequence to the theme from *Schindler's List*.

Classroom review

Ask the children what they enjoyed most about doing this dance. *What worked and what didn't? Why do you think that was?*

Assessing learning outcomes

Are the children able to remember and perform the dance in groups?

Lesson organisation
Brief classroom discussion; individual warm-up; development, dance and cool-down in pairs; teacher-led classroom review.

Vocabulary
stroll
limp
swagger
dodge
creep
saunter
strut
amble

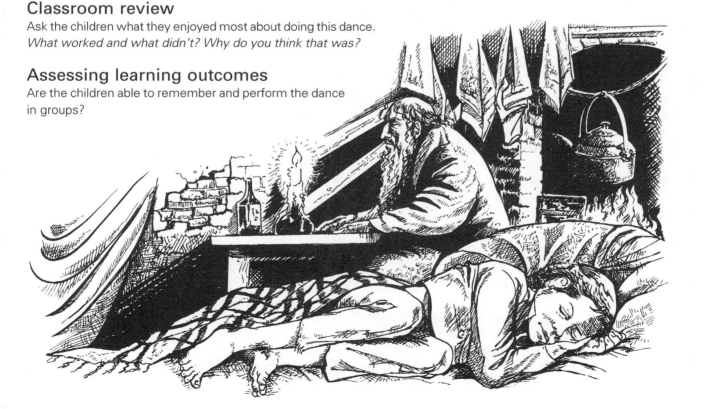

Gymnastics

In order to help children fully explore the potential of their bodies through gymnastics, it is necessary to suggest some challenges or place some limitations in movement. By providing a clear focus of attention, children can be involved in thinking about, performing and adapting their movements to the different suggestions. It is this response to movement problems which is so important. Children need time to play with ideas, to practise, consolidate and refine their favourite movements as well as to have new ones suggested to them. To explore the potential of different ideas and themes involves creativity, adaptation and review. Children are all individual and will come to each session with very different interests, past experiences, abilities and physiques. Progression, therefore, should be seen in a number of dimensions, not simply in the achievement of set gymnastic skills but also with increasing awareness of the body, of others and of safety, developing observational skills and increasing quality. Challenge is part of the interest and excitement, and a lot is dependent upon your interest and manner.

Symmetry and asymmetry

This unit gives particular emphasis to the shape of the body and the relationship of individual parts to the whole while travelling, in balance and in flight.

Partner work: linking actions

This unit provides opportunities for children to share, refine and combine their ideas to create a sequence and to broaden the challenge of actions in travelling, flight and balance.

The units of work

Exploration and development of these ideas in each unit of work will help children to increase their movement vocabulary in gymnastics by:

● encouraging and challenging them to find different solutions to the movement problems set
● trying specific suggested actions.

By developing a theme gradually over a series of lessons, children can be helped to build up both confidence and competence and be encouraged to respond imaginatively to the task. The limited focus will help the children to be clear about what they are trying to do and how they are doing it, as well as giving them scope for individual responses, whatever their ability.

Within each lesson, tasks have been selected for introduction or repetition as necessary, depending upon the children's responses. Attempts have been made to ensure that there is a balance between the introduction of new ideas and the choice and practise of familiar movements and parts of the body used. Demonstrations can be chosen from the children's responses to illustrate range of ideas (to increase variety), use of space, and quality.

Encourage the children to try several different ways and then to select actions from those practised which answer the task set. As part of the floor work and apparatus parts of the lesson, children can then be encouraged to refine their moves and to explore and practise different ways of linking them.

Apparatus

A variety of types of apparatus, fixed and portable are available. See photocopiable page 130 for sample apparatus layouts.

Storage and accessibility of apparatus

Children will enjoy taking responsibility for planning and handling the apparatus, but you will need to give them clear guidance and direction.

It is essential that resources are easily accessible and that clear routines for getting out and putting away apparatus are adopted. In Years 5 and 6, children who have had regular experience

of lifting, carrying and using apparatus could be involved in planning or helping to design arrangements of apparatus for their group.

Organisation of apparatus

Make a plan of the apparatus to be used, checking what equipment is available. Make sure that it will support the theme.

Divide the class into six groups (to ensure all children have a range of experiences and to help spacing). Each group should be responsible for handling the *same* apparatus throughout each unit.

Establish a fair and logical pattern of rotation of groups (for example, zigzag, clockwise or straight swap if there are groups with

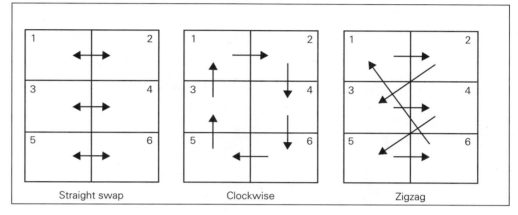

Straight swap   Clockwise   Zigzag

similar apparatus), so that over a period of several lessons, the children can have a range of experiences. (NB. There should be a maximum of two apparatus changes in one lesson.) The zigzag is recommended so that groups use different types of apparatus in any one lesson.

Alternatively, children could be encouraged to move freely to use different pieces or different combinations of apparatus.

Remind each group how to get out their apparatus (the correct positioning for carrying it; bending their knees, not their backs; all looking in the direction in which they are going), and where to put it. (Chalk marks can be used to indicate positioning of apparatus.)

Check the fixings and placement of all apparatus before it is used and encourage children to do this too.

Using apparatus

Whatever their previous experience, children will need to be taught or reminded to handle and use the apparatus carefully, with emphasis on the safety factors. There are two main methods for using the apparatus:

● Free use. Children get out and put away the same apparatus but they move freely around the whole area, working all the time and not standing waiting for turns. This gives children the opportunity to use their initiative and be independent in their choices.

● Groups. This is recommended, particularly when some apparatus are limited, such as ropes or climbing frames. Group organisation helps to ensure fair turns and will enable each group of children to have a similar amount of time on each arrangement. Each group will get out and put away their own apparatus but rotate to use other parts of the apparatus.

Whichever method you use:

● establish 'ground rules', for example, working quietly and considerately, using all the space, using the floor as well as the apparatus

● insist on a quiet working atmosphere, but discuss why this is important

● encourage and help children to share space and equipment (using the floor space around the apparatus), particularly when there is limited apparatus

● establish a consistent routine for stopping, coming down and sitting away from the apparatus after their practice.

Encourage the children to take responsibility for the safe handling, placement and checking of the apparatus, but it must always be checked by you too. To encourage maximum activity and independence and avoid queues, help the children to use their apparatus thoughtfully in different ways, sharing the space available and moving carefully, responsibly and imaginatively.

Handling the Cave Southampton apparatus

Children in Years 5 and 6 should have had some prior experience in getting out this apparatus, but will still need reminders. Allocate this responsibility to one group for a unit of work or series

Diagram 1

of lessons (half a term) so that they become proficient and confident in handling it.

Before using the apparatus, check that the sockets for location bolts are clear and that any attachments (such as poles and ladders) are accessible and safely placed.

Safety is essential and your explanation of the following procedure should focus on what should happen and why it is necessary.

● One child pulls down on each handle to release the frame (or trackway) and to lift it on to its wheels, keeping one hand on the handle and one hand on the frame (see Diagram 1). (NB. This must happen simultaneously with other linked panels.)

● It is not essential, but another child could join in to pull each panel out when you give the signal. Remind them to watch their toes as the frame is pulled backwards.

● The bolt is lined up with the hole and the frame is then bolted to the floor as the handle is lifted.

● The straining wire is pulled, tightened and then secured by hooking it onto the lever and pressing it down to keep it in place (see Diagram 2).

● Apparatus fixings are checked by you and the children.

● Ladders or poles can then be fixed to the main frame.

Diagram 2

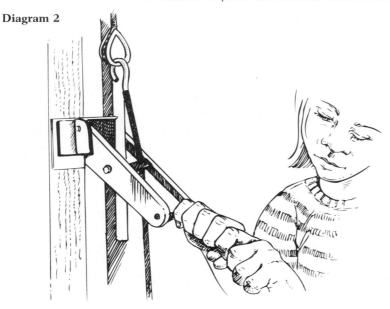

To put this apparatus away, the reverse procedure is adopted, checking that the bolt is resting in the wall bracket (top and bottom) to secure the frame against the wall for storage.

Three groups (of no more than 15 children) can use two panels of this apparatus (a bay each), provided that additional other pieces of apparatus (benches, mats and planks, poles, ladders) are added to help spacing. All the children will need reminders about spacing.

Two children can carry the poles (one at each end), but two further children are needed to hold the weight of the pole while the screws are tightened and secured in the holes in the frame.

Ladders can be carried on their sides and placed flat on the floor before being lifted and fixed to the bar at the required height.

Symmetry and asymmetry

The theme for this series of lessons will help children to clarify and refine the symmetrical and asymmetrical shapes that they can make with their bodies:

- in balance
- while travelling on different parts of their body
- in flight.

The focus on symmetry to begin with will help children select actions with which they are familiar and in which both sides of the body are matching. The travelling actions will be limited to forward and back or up and down directions, but the main purpose for the focus on shape is to help the children be more precise with their actions. The opportunities to practise symmetrical balances will help the class to refine the shape of these actions and be more controlled in the performance. The focus on symmetry in flight will help children to refine the actions that take them off the ground.

Once the class have explored and practised a number of symmetrical actions, a contrast can be introduced by drawing the children's attention to balances or travelling actions when the body is asymmetrical. The concentration will still be on body awareness, refining and clarifying actions with the emphasis on each side of the body doing different things (for example one limb forward one back, one bent one stretched).

Some ideas for symmetrical and asymmetrical positions using both the floor and apparatus are provided on photocopiable pages 131–3. Guidance for some different ways of travelling by rolling for linking balances is given on photocopiable page 135.

For the first, and then subsequent lessons, tasks can be carefully selected to initiate and stimulate ideas from the children. Tasks can be introduced or repeated as necessary, depending on how the children respond. It is important that there is a balance between:

- the introduction of new ideas and the choice and practise of familiar movements
- moving and still positions
- parts of the body used (not all one lesson just on feet or rolling, for example – equally not every possible body part used in one lesson).

Select from the children's responses when appropriate to demonstrate variations in their movement ideas, for example two or three children using similar body parts but making different shapes.

Give the children ample time to repeat, practise and consolidate positions, to refine their movements and build up their confidence and competence.

The unit is divided into six sessions allowing 30–40 minutes of activity per session. Each session will involve both floor and apparatus work, but ideas can be modified to suit your school context.

The class could be divided into six groups to ensure good spacing and fair turns on each group of apparatus (see the suggested apparatus plan on photocopiable page 130).

It is presumed that children will have already experienced different ways of travelling and balancing on different parts of the body.

UNIT: Symmetry and asymmetry

Enquiry questions	Learning objectives	Teaching activities	Learning outcomes
Which gymnastics actions are symmetrical?	● Introduce and develop the concept and actions involved in symmetry. ● Practise ways of making symmetrical balanced shapes on the floor and on apparatus. ● Explore, develop and refine ways of travelling symmetrically on both feet and on parts of the body using both floor and apparatus.	Warm-up: skipping or hopping using different directions; trying other travelling actions clarifying the shapes; selecting symmetrical actions. Development: practising ways of travelling on feet keeping the body symmetrical; balancing in a symmetrical shape using different parts of the body; refining symmetrical shapes; selecting and linking two ways of travelling on feet symmetrically and two symmetrical balances. Apparatus work: trying ways of travelling symmetrically towards, away from, along or around the apparatus; trying symmetrical balances on different parts of the apparatus; practising and linking favourite symmetrical balances and travelling actions on the apparatus. Cool-down: jogging on the spot; practising a shoulder stand with legs in different symmetrical positions lowering legs to kneel, jumping to finish.	Children: ● understand symmetrical shapes ● control their balances ● clarify the shapes of their symmetrical travelling actions
Can we improve our symmetrical shapes and actions?	● Refine the shapes of balances using symmetrical shapes on both floor and apparatus. ● Develop further ways of travelling using hands and feet symmetrically, on both the floor and on the apparatus. ● Introduce rotational symmetry. ● Practise ways of jumping with a symmetrical shape, on the floor and low apparatus.	Warm-up: leaping and jumping with clear shapes and good landings; practising still symmetrical shapes. Development: practising different ways of jumping making a symmetrical shape in the air; trying still, symmetrical shapes on hands or hands and feet; travelling symmetrically on hands and feet; practising rotational symmetry; practising two ways of travelling on hands and feet symmetrically and two symmetrical balances on hands and feet. Apparatus work: practising symmetrical travelling actions on, along or around the apparatus; practising symmetrical balances on hands and feet using floor and apparatus; trying ideas for rotational symmetry and practising symmetrical balances and travelling actions on the apparatus; trying ideas on next apparatus. Cool-down: jogging on the spot; practising a bottom balance with legs in different symmetrical positions, returning to standing.	● refine their symmetrical actions ● understand rotational symmetry ● are imaginative in their responses
Which gymnastics actions are asymmetrical?	● Explore ways of travelling on feet and jumping asymmetrically on the floor and apparatus. ● Explore ways of using hands and feet to move asymmetrically. ● Explore ways of balancing asymmetrically.	Warm-up: travelling sideways in different ways and refining actions; linking three ways of moving asymmetrically on feet; trying still asymmetrical shapes. Development: practising different ways of jumping asymmetrically; refining shapes; trying different asymmetrical balances on hands or hands and feet; travelling on feet or hands and feet asymmetrically; practising two ways of travelling on hands and feet asymmetrically and two asymmetrical balances on hands and feet. Apparatus work: trying asymmetrical travelling actions on, along or around the apparatus; trying asymmetrical balances on hands and feet on different parts of the apparatus; practising favourite asymmetrical balances and travelling actions on the apparatus. Cool-down: walking, relaxing arms; practising bottom or shoulder balance with legs in asymmetrical positions, lowering legs and relaxing.	● distinguish between asymmetry and symmetry in their actions ● clarify their asymmetrical shapes

Enquiry questions	Learning objectives	Teaching activities	Learning outcomes
Can we improve our asymmetrical shapes and actions?	● Practise ways of travelling asymmetrically on feet and hands and feet on the floor and apparatus. ● Refine the shapes of asymmetrical jumps. ● Try out other asymmetrical balance actions on the floor and on different parts of the apparatus. ● Begin to link some of the travelling and balancing actions together.	Warm-up: travelling in different ways changing direction or level; practising still symmetrical or asymmetrical shapes. Development: trying ways of moving on hands and feet asymmetrically; practising different ways of jumping asymmetrically; refining the asymmetrical shapes; showing and helping a partner; practising still asymmetrical shapes on hands or hands and feet; travelling on hands and feet asymmetrically; practising and linking two ways of travelling symmetrically and two ways of travelling asymmetrically. Apparatus work: practising asymmetrical travelling actions on, along or around the apparatus; practising asymmetrical balances on hands and feet using different parts of the apparatus; linking actions together. Cool-down: hopping then practising an asymmetrical balance on one leg.	● refine their actions, particularly their jumps ● make use of all parts of the apparatus in imaginative ways
Can we make a sequence of these actions?	● Select and practise special symmetrical and asymmetrical actions to put into a floor sequence. ● Select and try different ways of linking them together. ● Select and practise special symmetrical and asymmetrical actions on the apparatus.	Warm-up: travelling in different ways changing direction and level of travel; practising a still symmetrical then asymmetrical shape; practising leaping. Development: practising different ways of jumping asymmetrically; refining asymmetrical shapes; practising asymmetrical balances on hands or hands and feet; travelling on hands and feet asymmetrically; linking together travelling symmetrically and two ways of travelling asymmetrically smoothly; adding a starting and finishing position. Apparatus work: practising symmetrical travelling and jumping actions; practising symmetrical balances on hands and feet; practising symmetrical and asymmetrical balances, jumps and travelling actions and ways of linking them together. Cool-down: jogging slowly; practising balancing on one leg in an asymmetrical position.	● select appropriate actions ● try different ways to link their movements together
How can we improve our sequences?	● Practise sequences on the floor and on the apparatus, demonstrating symmetry and asymmetry. ● Refine the actions, linking them together as smoothly as possible with starting and finishing positions.	Warm-up: travelling around the hall in different ways, changing direction then level; practising different ways of jumping; demonstrating a still symmetrical/asymmetrical shape. Development: refining ways of jumping and leaping asymmetrically; practising asymmetrical balances and travelling actions on hands or hands and feet; linking together symmetrical and asymmetrical actions. Apparatus work: refining symmetrical travelling actions and balances on the apparatus linking them together. Cool-down: jogging on the spot; practising an asymmetrical balance.	● demonstrate their knowledge of symmetry and asymmetry by linking their chosen actions into a sequence ● describe their symmetrical and asymmetrical actions.

Cross-curricular links
Maths: discussion and previous work in the classroom will have introduced children to symmetrical and asymmetrical shapes. This theme will enhance children's understanding of these shapes by encouraging them to select and refine their actions. Through contexts in PE which are familiar, through trying out and investigating with their own bodies and through describing what they have done, children will develop a greater understanding of these concepts. A focus on rotational symmetry will help children to appreciate and understand movement around an axis or centre.

Resources
Gymnastic apparatus; photocopiable pages 130–5.

Display
Symmetrical and asymmetrical shapes for maths, and photographs of children's ideas in gymnastics, enlarged copies of photocopiable pages 131–3.

(35 mins) Which gymnastics actions are symmetrical?

Learning objectives
● Introduce and develop the concept and actions involved in symmetry.
● Practise ways of making symmetrical balanced shapes on the floor and on apparatus.
● Explore, develop and refine ways of travelling symmetrically on both feet and on parts of the body using both floor and apparatus.

Lesson organisation
Classroom introduction; individual exercises; apparatus work in six groups; individual cool-down; teacher-led classroom review.

Vocabulary
refine
forwards
backwards
up
down
shoulder stand
jump
travel
bottom balance

What you need and preparation

Discuss with the children in the classroom the special requirements for getting out the apparatus (see Apparatus in the chapter introduction) and discuss symmetry. Using photocopiable page 134, cut and fold the template to illustrate that the sides of the body are symmetrical and that this is what they should be aiming for in their postitions.

Organise the children into six groups (of approximately five children) and allocate apparatus to each one (see photocopiable page 130 for a sample layout).

What to do

(5 mins) Warm-up

Ensure that the children are well spaced to start the warm-up. Ask them to skip or hop around the hall and to refine their actions (pointing their toes, lifting their knees up, using light footwork). Encourage use of all the space, good use of different directions and high quality actions. Keep them moving until their pulse is raised.

Tell them to perform a strong push up with the legs and remind them to make good use of their arms to aid the action.

Ask them to try other travelling actions on their feet, clarifying the shape of them. Observe the responses and select one way of moving with two feet together, for example, squat jumps, for everyone to try.

(14 mins) Development

In their own space, ask the children to try and practise other ways of travelling on their feet, keeping their bodies symmetrical. Encourage variations of arm position and level and check for forward and backward directions.

Ask the class to show you different ways of balancing in a symmetrical shape. Tell everyone to practise several ways, then encourage them all to use different parts of their bodies. For example, lying on backs or fronts, shoulder stands, bottom balances, headstands (see Diagram 3) and so on. Encourage keeping body shape and tension and help the children to refine their symmetrical shapes. Ask the children for demonstrations to illustrate two or three ways.

Ask the children to try some of the ways they have seen or some different ways of their own. Emphasise the symmetrical aspects.

Now let everyone select two ways of travelling on their feet symmetrically and two symmetrical balances on different parts of their bodies, and to begin to link them together.

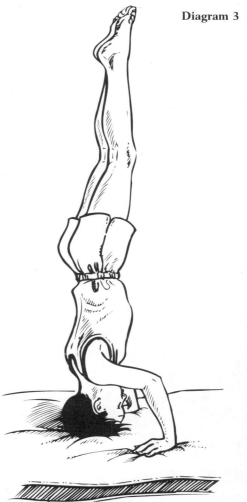

Diagram 3

14 mins **Apparatus work**
Referring to the notes in the chapter introduction and the sample apparatus plan on photocopiable page 130, ask the six groups to get out their allocated apparatus. Use apparatus cards for this if appropriate.

Ask the children to try out ways of travelling symmetrically towards, away from, along, or around the apparatus. Insist that they look for spaces and encourage them to keep moving.

Ask the class to try out some of the symmetrical balances on different parts of the apparatus, on bottoms, tummies or hands for example. Encourage imaginative use of the floor and apparatus (on it , against it , under it and so on). Look for examples of the different possibilities to use as demonstrations and suggest ideas to other children.

Allow everyone to select and practise their favourite or interesting symmetrical balances and travelling actions on the apparatus. Can they start to link them together?

To finish, ask the groups to put their own apparatus away carefully.

2 mins **Cool-down**
Tell all the children to jog lightly on the spot.

Ask them to practise a shoulder stand, moving their legs into different symmetrical positions. Tell them to repeat this, lowering their legs down and putting their knees to the side and to move to a kneeling position. Tell them then to push on their hands to get back on their feet with a jump to finish.

Classroom review
In pairs, or as a whole class, encourage the children to describe some of the symmetrical actions they tried during the lesson.

Assessing learning outcomes
Do all of the children understand symmetrical shapes? Are they controlling their balances? Are they clarifying the shapes of their symmetrical travelling actions?

35 mins Can we improve our symmetrical shapes and actions?

What you need and preparation
Remind the children of the requirements for getting out and using the apparatus. Discuss symmetry, particularly rotational symmetry, and talk about how this can be applied in gymnastics, for example in performing a cart-wheel.

What to do
4 mins **Warm-up**
Ask the children to travel around the hall, practising leaping (taking off from one foot and landing on the other) and then jumping (taking off from one foot or two feet and landing on two). Prompt them to refine their actions, with light footwork and resilient landings. Encourage use of all the space, good use of different directions and quality actions. Continue this for a short while, until pulses are raised.

Ask the children to stop occasionally to demonstrate a still symmetrical shape. Encourage stretching in this position and good body tension.

Learning objectives
● Refine the shapes of balances using symmetrical shapes on both floor and apparatus.
● Develop further ways of travelling using hands and feet symmetrically, on both the floor and on the apparatus.
● Introduce rotational symmetry.
● Practise ways of jumping with a symmetrical shape, on the floor and low apparatus.

Lesson organisation
Classroom discussion; individual exercises; apparatus work in six groups; individual cool-down; teacher-led classroom review.

Symmetry and
asymmetry

Diagram 4

12 **Development**
mins Ask the class to practise different ways of jumping and then to concentrate on making a symmetrical shape in the air, landing with two feet together. Encourage them to try different symmetrical shapes (for example star, tuck, straddle pike – see Diagram 4) and then to refine the symmetry.

Use demonstrations to illustrate two or three ways. Then ask all the children to try some different ways. Remind them to think about symmetry in their actions.

Ask everyone to try still symmetrical shapes on their hands or hands and feet. Encourage them to select their favourites and to practise and refine them.

Next, ask them to travel on their hands and feet, keeping their bodies symmetrical (such as a bunny jump or cat spring).

Remind the class of rotational symmetry and ask everyone to try moving sideways, keeping the body symmetrical. Suggest a sideways log roll or cart-wheel action.

Ask the children to select and practise two ways of travelling on hands and feet symmetrically and then two symmetrical balances on hands and feet.

If there is time, ask them to work in pairs to observe and help each other clarify the symmetrical jumps, travelling actions and balanced shapes.

Vocabulary
symmetry
axis
rotational
symmetry
clarify
balance
quality
leap
jump
tension
log roll
cart-wheel
bunny jump
cat spring

16 **Apparatus work**
mins Ask the groups to get out their apparatus and move to the next set up they are to work on.

Let the children practise some of their favourite symmetrical travelling actions on, along or around the apparatus. Check their spacing as you observe.

Ask the class to try out some of the symmetrical balances on hands and feet, using different parts of the apparatus. Encourage imaginative use of the floor and pieces of apparatus and ask a few children to demonstrate good balances.

Ask all the children to find places on the floor, mat or apparatus where they can move sideways, keeping the body symmetrical. For example, a cart-wheel action could be tried across a mat, bench or low plank. Emphasise having wide arms and legs.

Let everyone select and practise their symmetrical balances and travelling actions on the apparatus.

To finish, tell them to rotate to the next apparatus and try these tasks on the new apparatus. Then ask the groups to put away their apparatus.

3 **Cool-down**
mins Ask the children to space out and jog on the spot lightly with their heads up.

Then ask them to practise a few bottom balances, with their legs in different symmetrical positions. Encourage them to practise different ways of returning to their feet to finish.

Classroom review
Ask the children to describe some of the symmetrical actions they tried during the session. Discuss these and give examples of rotational symmetry.

Assessing learning outcomes
Are the children able to think of and practise ways of refining their symmetrical actions? Do they understand rotational symmetry? Are they imaginative in their responses?

(35 mins) Which gymnastics actions are asymmetrical?

What you need and preparation

You will need apparatus for six groups.

Remind the class of the particular requirements for getting out apparatus, and check the rotation of the groups on the apparatus. Revise asymmetry in maths and introduce it in relation to gymnastics.

What to do

(5 mins) Warm-up

Ask the children to travel around the hall sideways. Encourage them to try different ways and then refine their actions. Remind them to keep their footwork light and move in both directions. Encourage them to use all the space and maintain good quality actions. Keep the children moving until their pulses are raised, but ask them to stop occasionally to demonstrate a still asymmetrical shape.

Ask them to select three ways of moving asymmetrically on their feet and to start to link them together (for example hop, run and leap).

(14 mins) Development

Ask the class to practise different ways of jumping, making an asymmetrical shape in the air, but still landing with two feet together. Encourage them to try different shapes (for example one arm up and one down; one leg forward and one back, one limb stretched and one bent). Encourage and help them to be precise about the position of their limbs and to refine their asymmetrical shapes.

Ask a couple of children doing this well to illustrate two or three ways. Then ask everyone to try some different ways. Emphasise the asymmetrical aspects.

Now tell the children to try some different asymmetrical balances on their hands or hands and feet (see Diagram 5, for example). Let them select their favourites to practise and refine.

Ask the children to travel on their feet or hands and feet, keeping their bodies asymmetrical. Watch as they choose and practise two ways of travelling on their hands and feet asymmetrically and two asymmetrical balances on hands and feet.

Learning objectives
● Explore ways of travelling on feet and jumping asymmetrically on the floor and apparatus.
● Explore ways of using hands and feet to move asymmetrically.
● Explore ways of balancing asymmetrically.

Lesson organisation
Classroom discussion; individual exercises; apparatus work in six groups; individual cool-down; teacher-led classroom review.

Diagram 5

**Symmetry and
asymmetry**

Vocabulary
symmetry
asymmetry
refine
improve
clarify
travelling action
balance
jump

Apparatus work

14 mins Begin by asking the groups to get out and set up their apparatus and then rotate to use the next arrangement.

Ask everyone to try some asymmetrical travelling actions on, along or around the apparatus. Check that they are spacing out well.

Ask the class to try out some of the asymmetrical balances on hands and feet, using different parts of the apparatus. Encourage imaginative use of the floor and apparatus. Remind them of *on*, *against*, *under* and so on (see Diagram 6).

Look for examples of the different possibilities to suggest ideas to other children. Then let everyone select and practise their favourite asymmetrical balances and travelling actions on the apparatus.

To finish, ask the groups to rotate to the next apparatus and try the tasks again, before putting their apparatus away.

Diagram 6

Cool-down

2 mins Ask all the children to walk around the space, relaxing their arms.

Then ask them to practise a bottom balance or shoulder balance, with their legs in asymmetrical positions (see Diagram 7), and then to lower their legs down until they are in a lying position.

Classroom review

Encourage the children to describe the asymmetrical actions they tried. Ask: *How can you remember them for next week?*

Assessing learning outcomes

Can the children distinguish between asymmetry and symmetry in their actions? Are they able to clarify their asymmetrical shapes?

Diagram 7

(35 mins) Can we improve our asymmetrical shapes and actions?

What you need and preparation

You will need apparatus for the six groups.

In the classroom, talk with the children about the special requirements for getting out the apparatus (see Apparatus on page 34) and revise asymmetry.

What to do

(5 mins) Warm-up

Ensure the children are well spaced to start the warm-up. Ask them to travel around the hall in different ways and on your *Change* signal, to change their direction or level of travel. Ask them to try several different ways and then refine their actions, keeping their footwork light. Look for good use of the space and quality actions. Keep them moving until pulses are raised.

Ask the children to stop on your signal to choose and demonstrate a still symmetrical or asymmetrical shape.

Diagram 8

(14 mins) Development

Ask the class to practise different ways of jumping in the air in an asymmetrical shape (see Diagram 8), landing with feet together. Encourage them to choose two or three different shapes and clarify the position of the arms and legs.

Encourage and help the children to refine their asymmetrical shapes, helping each other in pairs. Can they repeat the shape to show their partners later?

Use demonstrations to illustrate two or three ways, emphasising the asymmetrical aspects.

Ask the children, on their own, to practise asymmetrical shapes on their hands or hands and feet. Encourage them to select their favourites and to refine these balances. Emphasise good body tension and help them to hold their balances for a count of three.

Now ask everyone to travel on their hands and feet using their bodies asymmetrically. Encourage them to select two ways of travelling symmetrically and two ways of travelling asymmetrically and to practise them.

Organise the children into pairs and ask them to observe their partners and help them to refine their actions.

Then, individually, see how well everyone can refine their actions and begin linking them together smoothly.

(14 mins) Apparatus work

In their six groups, ask the children to get out their apparatus and rotate to use the next arrangement.

Ask them to practise asymmetrical travelling actions on, along or around the apparatus. Check their spacing.

Ask the class to try out some of the asymmetrical balances on their hands and feet using different parts of the apparatus. Encourage imaginative use of the floor and apparatus (on it, against it and under it). Choose a few children to demonstrate some of the different possibilities and use these demonstrations to suggest ideas to the other children.

Let everyone select and practise their favourite asymmetrical balances and travelling actions on the apparatus. Encourage them to use different parts of their bodies and to start to think of ways of linking these actions together.

Then ask the groups to rotate to their next apparatus to try these tasks on the new arrangement.

 Cool-down

Tell all the children to hop on the spot, first on one leg, then the other.

Ask them to practise a balance on one leg with an asymmetrical shape, then stretch and relax to finish.

Classroom review

Encourage the children to record the asymmetrical actions they tried today and to start to think which ones they might include in a sequence.

Assessing learning outcomes

Are the children able to refine their actions, particularly their jumps? Are they making use of all parts of the apparatus in imaginative ways?

(35 mins) Can we make a sequence of these actions?

Learning objectives
● Select and practise special symmetrical and asymmetrical actions to put into a floor sequence.
● Try different ways of linking them together.
● Select and practise special symmetrical and asymmetrical actions on the apparatus.

Lesson organisation
Classroom discussion; individual exercises; apparatus work in six groups; individual cool-down; teacher-led classroom review.

What you need and preparation

You will need apparatus for the six groups, accessible around the sides of the hall.

Before going to the hall, talk together about the particular requirements for setting up and using apparatus (see Apparatus on page 34).

Revise symmetry and asymmetry, asking the children to think which symmetrical and asymmetrical actions they might choose for a sequence.

What to do

 Warm-up

Ensure the children are well spaced to start the warm-up.

Ask them to stride around the hall in different ways and on the *Change* signal, to alter their direction of travel. Encourage them to try several different ways of jumping and then to refine their actions, trying to be more precise in their actions. Encourage everyone to use all of the space and maintain good quality actions. Continue until their pulses are raised.

Invite the children to practise their favourite still, symmetrical or asymmetrical shapes. Then ask them to practise leaping, and as they do so, to think about the shapes they are making in the air.

Development

Ask the class to practise different ways of jumping, making asymmetrical shapes in the air, landing with their feet together. Encourage them to try a variety of different shapes and to clarify the positions of their arms and legs.

Encourage and help the children to refine their asymmetrical shapes, and use demonstrations to illustrate two or three examples. Ask the whole class to repeat and refine their actions, emphasising the asymmetry.

Diagram 9

Ask the children to try one, then other, asymmetrical balances on their hands (see Diagram 9, for example) or hands and feet. Encourage them to choose their favourites, and to practise and refine those particular shapes.

Tell the children to travel on their hands and feet, using their bodies asymmetrically. Encourage them to select two ways of travelling symmetrically and two ways of travelling asymmetrically and to practise all four a few times.

Now help them to link these actions together smoothly, making the end of one movement become the beginning of the next. Can they add a starting and finishing position? Encourage them to change the order of the actions to see which order helps the continuity of the sequence.

(15 mins) Apparatus work

Ask the children to get out their apparatus and then to rotate to the next arrangement.

Ask them to practise some of their favourite symmetrical travelling actions on, along or around the apparatus. Check that the children are maintaining space between them. Prompt them to think about their actions by asking: *Can you find different places where you can jump? Which movement will you do when you have landed?*

Observe as the children try out some of the symmetrical balances on their hands and feet using different parts of the apparatus. How do they lower themselves or move out of the balance into the next move? Look for good examples of the different possibilities and use demonstrations to encourage the rest of the children.

Invite everyone to select and practise symmetrical and asymmetrical balances, jumps and travelling actions on the apparatus. Encourage them to use different parts of the apparatus and link their balances together. Ask: *Where will you start? Which action could you do towards or away from the apparatus? Where will you balance?* Ask them to practise different combinations and pathways and to remember their favourites.

Tell the groups to rotate to the next apparatus to repeat the above exercises.

(2 mins) Cool-down

Ask all the children to jog slowly about the space. Then tell them to practise a balance on one leg, in an asymmetrical position, and then to try another, different shape.

Classroom review

Encourage the children to describe the asymmetrical actions they tried during the lesson. What did they particularly enjoy? Did they find anything very difficult?

Assessing learning outcomes

Are the children selecting appropriate actions? Are they trying different ways to link their movements together?

CHAPTER 2 GYMNASTICS

Symmetry and asymmetry

Learning objectives
● Practise sequences on the floor and apparatus, demonstrating symmetry and asymmetry.
● Refine actions, linking them together smoothly, with starting and finishing positions.

Lesson organisation
Classroom discussion; individual warm-up; individual and paired exercises; apparatus work in groups; individual cool-down; teacher-led classroom review.

Vocabulary
symmetry
asymmetry
jump
sequence
linking
refine
clarify
smooth
balance
axis

What you need and preparation

You will need apparatus for the six groups.

Revise symmetry and asymmetry before going to the hall.

What to do

(5 mins) Warm-up

Begin by asking everyone to travel around the hall in different ways. Use a *Change* signal to prompt a change of direction or level of travel. Encourage the children to try several different ways and then refine their actions, keeping moving until their pulses are raised.

Ask them to practise some different ways of jumping. Remind them to consider their landings and clarify the shapes in the air.

(12 mins) Development

Ask the class to refine two ways of jumping, making an asymmetrical shape in the air, landing with both feet together; and one leap, landing one foot after the other. Encourage the children to try asymmetrical shapes and to refine new jumps, encouraging each other in pairs.

Use demonstrations to illustrate the asymmetrical aspects of the shapes.

Invite everyone to refine their favourite asymmetrical shapes on their hands or hands and feet.

Ask the children to travel on their hands and feet, using their bodies asymmetrically as they move. Tell them to select and practise two ways of travelling symmetrically and two ways of travelling asymmetrically.

Ask them to take it in turns to observe a partner and to comment on their sequences and how well they link them together. Then ask the children to practise individually, taking into account the comments they have received.

(15 mins) Apparatus work

Referring to the apparatus notes and the sample plan on page 130, ask the children to get out and set up their apparatus, then move to the arrangement on which they are to work.

Ask the children to practise some of their favourite symmetrical travelling actions on, along, or around the apparatus. Check their spacing.

Then ask them to try out some of the symmetrical balances on their hands and feet using different parts of the apparatus. Encourage imaginative use of the floor and apparatus. Remind them of *on*, *against* and *under*. Look for different possibilities for demonstrations and use these to suggest ideas to other children.

Invite everyone to choose and practise their favourite asymmetrical balances and travelling actions on the apparatus and to link them together.

(3 mins) Cool-down

Ask all the children to jog lightly on the spot, then practise an asymmetrical balance.

Classroom review

Ask the children to say what they liked about some of the sequences they observed.

Assessing learning outcomes

Can the children demonstrate their knowledge of symmetry and asymmetry by linking their chosen actions into a sequence? Can they describe their symmetrical and asymmetrical actions?

Partner work: linking actions

The focus for this series of lessons will introduce children to different ways of working with a partner to devise and perform a gymnastic sequence. Although partner work can be used as an extension to most themes, it is presumed that earlier in their primary schooling children will have had some experience of working with a partner – matching, mirroring or following a leader.

Partner work is both challenging and exciting and it is used here in its own right and as a focus for linking actions. Much 'give and take', trust and responsibility are needed as children learn to share their ideas, rely on their partners and select movements appropriately. To work with someone else in a gymnastic context requires careful observation and planning, sensitivity and lots of adjustment, but it can also be an opportunity for children to try actions which are impossible to do alone.

These lessons will help children to:
● clarify and refine their skills
● develop control and precision in their actions
● practise ways of linking actions and combining these with a partner
● collaborate to create or compose a sequence
● trust and take responsibility for a partner
● observe, describe, discuss, negotiate, evaluate and make judgements, individually and together
● raise their awareness of shape, timing and spacing
● begin to appreciate aesthetic principles
● select and design an apparatus layout in groups
● help each other use the apparatus safely and imaginatively.

Four particular aspects of partner work will be introduced to provide a vocabulary of ideas for the sequences:
● using a partner as an obstacle – under, over around without and with touching, with matching or contrasting shapes
● assisted flight
● counterbalance
● counter tension.

Some positions for counterbalance are suggested on photocopiable page 136. Reminders for how to perform rolls, on photocopiable page 135, would also be useful for these lessons.

Each of these aspects can be explored and developed more fully to allow children time to really experiment with ideas and to be creative and adjust to collaborating with a partner.

The unit will raise children's awareness of the different ways they can work with their partners and help them to incorporate variations in shape, level, direction and speed in their sequences. Each lesson will involve 30–45 minutes of activity.

UNIT: Partner work: linking actions

Enquiry questions	Learning objectives	Teaching activities	Learning outcomes
Can we use our partners as obstacles?	• Revise ways of following and matching a partner. • Practise and refine ways of balancing and jumping individually, on the floor and apparatus. • Explore ways of moving over and under a partner. • Explore ways of linking actions and combining them with a partner on the floor and apparatus.	Warm-up: jogging using different pathways; jogging in pairs synchronising the steps; practising a variety of jumps individually, then clarifying shapes and timing with a partner; stretching in pairs. Floor work: practising favourite gymnastic moves; practising low balances; travelling to a new space to balance; lowering from balance to move on; in pairs one balancing, one moving around the partner; one making a low shape and the partner jumping over it; trying matching shapes and contrasting shapes; combining travel and balance in pairs. Apparatus work: jumping off apparatus; balancing on, against or beside apparatus; helping a partner to land; exploring ways of jumping over a partner; moving around or under a partner; linking some actions together. Cool-down: practising trust fall with a partner; shaking, stretching and relaxing.	Children: • clarify their actions • work well with their partners
Can we move over our partners while they are moving?	• Practise and refine jumps and balances, individually and in pairs. • Explore ways of jumping and moving over a partner – as both a still and a moving obstacle. • Explore contrasting and matching shapes with a partner. • Introduce assisted flight. • Select and practise ways of moving over or under a partner on the apparatus.	Warm-up: skipping using different directions; synchronising skipping steps with a partner; individually then with a partner refining favourite jumps; stretching. Floor work: in pairs practising ways of balancing and rolling; practising balances for a partner to move around or under or over; trying contrasting and matching shapes; trying other ways of moving over a partner; introducing assisted flight – helping a partner to jump upwards. Apparatus work: practising jumps from apparatus; helping a partner to jump and land; balancing while a partner jumps over or moves under the shape; practising two or three favourite ways; linking them in a different order smoothly. Cool-down: practising trust falls with a partner; shaking, stretching and relaxing.	• look after their partners as they jump • begin to refine their ideas
Can we help our partners to jump?	• Practise ways of leaping and jumping individually and in pairs, assisting partner's flight. • Introduce and practise the leap-frog action. • Practise floor sequences in pairs, taking responsibility for each other. • Explore ways of linking actions.	Warm-up: running in different directions then running and leaping; practising different jumps (star and straddle); trying other shapes then the stag leap; stretching in pairs. Floor work: practising balances then ways of travelling on hands and feet individually; practising different ways of jumping with a partner; trying a leap-frog action; practising stable bases; practising leaping and running and jumping supporting a partner; trying ways of moving over a partner on all fours; linking ideas in a sequence. Apparatus work: practising ways of balancing individually then with a partner; practising leap-frog and other ideas using the apparatus; linking some partner actions using the apparatus. Cool-down: practising shoulder stands matching partner; stretching and relaxing.	• refine their jumps • support their partners • are careful

Enquiry questions	Learning objectives	Teaching activities	Learning outcomes
Can we balance with our partners?	● Practise turning jumps individually and with a partner. ● Introduce counterbalance. ● Work collaboratively with and trust a partner. ● Practise floor sequences in pairs.	Warm-up: jogging and then side-stepping individually then with a partner; stretching with a partner; practising turning jumps individually; practising ways of assisting a partner to jump. Floor work: practising turning jumps then supporting a partner in different ways; introduce counterbalance; practising taking partner's weight to lower to the ground; practising ways to complete the move; travelling away from a partner to balance; trying different starting positions; trying different ways of getting out of the balance. Apparatus work: practising ways of jumping with a partner; balancing for a partner to move over or under them; practising counterbalance ideas on the apparatus. Cool-down: practising shoulder stands with contrasting shapes to a partner; stretching and relaxing.	● trust and support each other ● lean against their partners to balance
Can we lean or push against our partners to balance?	● Introduce movements involving counter resistance. ● Practise and refine floor sequences in pairs. ● Devise and practise a sequence in pairs on the apparatus.	Warm-up: jogging and jumping in different directions taking turns to be leader; making a shape for a partner to move over to take the lead; refining selected ways of assisting a partner to jump. Floor work: moving over a partner; practising ideas for counterbalance with a partner; pushing, propping up or leaning against a partner; linking actions with a partner. Apparatus work: practising with a partner using apparatus; linking actions; practising how to start and finish sequences; selecting at least two balances and two assisted-flight actions to incorporate into a sequence; practising sequences in pairs on the apparatus. Cool-down: holding hands, pulling away from a partner to lower to the ground; stretching out and relaxing.	● think carefully about their starting and finishing positions ● work well together
How can we improve our paired sequences?	● Perform floor sequences in pairs. ● Refine a sequence in pairs on the apparatus. ● Comment and evaluate own work with a partner. ● Appreciate and acknowledge the work of others.	Warm-up: jumping individually and then in pairs. Floor work: practising different ways of balancing with a partner (counter resistance); including counterbalance and counter tension in sequences; performing floor sequences in pairs; observing and evaluating. Apparatus work: practising with a partner, using apparatus; including balances and two assisted flight actions in a sequence; practising sequences in pairs on the apparatus; practising the start and finish; watching and helping another pair to refine their actions; performing sequences in pairs on the apparatus. Cool-down: sitting back to back with a partner, pushing to stand up then lowering; lying, stretching and relaxing, breathing deeply.	● compose and practise their sequences on the floor and apparatus ● link actions together smoothly.

Cross-curricular links
Science: examining counterbalance and counter tension; pushing and pulling to maintain stability.

Resources
Low gymnastics apparatus – benches, box-tops, planks, trestle tabels, mats; photocopiable pages 135 and 136; writing materials; paper.

Display
Photographs of children's partner work actions; an enlarged copy of photocopiable page 136.

Partner work:
linking actions

(40 mins) Can we use our partners as obstacles?

Learning objectives
● Revise ways of following and matching a partner.
● Practise and refine ways of balancing and jumping, individually on the floor apparatus.
● Explore and practise ways of moving over and under a partner.
● Explore ways of linking actions and combining them with a partner on the floor and apparatus.

Lesson organisation
Brief classroom discussion; warm-up individually and in pairs; floor work in pairs; apparatus work individually and in pairs; cool-down in pairs; teacher-led classroom review.

What you need and preparation
You will need low apparatus (benches, box-tops, low planks, trestle tables and mats, *not* climbing apparatus); writing materials; paper.

Discuss with the class the special arrangements for doing gymnastics – appropriate clothing, getting to the hall and, especially, safe ways of working with a partner. Remind them of the procedures for using apparatus. If necessary, two pairs can share one piece of apparatus.

What to do

(6 mins) Warm-up
In a space, ask the class to jog gently all around the space using different pathways, trying to point their toes to the ground. Then ask them to try this in pairs, with one leading and one following, trying to synchronise the steps. To prompt their ideas, ask: *Can you try this side by side and still synchronise the steps? Which foot do you start with?* Ensure that the children take turns to be leader.

Ask the children to practise individually some of their favourite jumps and ask them what they need to remember to do to make sure their landings are resilient – bend their knees. Encourage variety by drawing attention to different shapes (twisted, curled, asymmetrical and so on).

With their partners, ask them to show each other three differently shaped jumps and to practise them together. Can they copy them exactly? Can they jump at the same time? Make a point of asking them to practise a tuck jump (bringing their knees to their chest rather than chest to knees – see Diagram 10).

Diagram 10

Now ask each of them to sit facing a partner with their legs wide apart, and to hold hands. One of them leans backwards slowly, thus pulling the other one forward to stretch (see Diagram 11). They hold the position for five seconds and then the other partner leans back, pulling his or her partner forward to stretch.

(18 mins) Floor work
On their own, let the children select and practise some of their other favourite gymnastic moves (for example a cart-wheel, shoulder balance, cat spring).

Then invite them to select and practise some low balances where their bodies stay near to the floor. Encourage them to use hands and feet (both hands and one foot; front or back support) as well as other

Diagram 11

**Partner work:
linking actions**

Vocabulary
pathways
synchronise
tucked
twisted
curled
asymmetrical
pulling

parts of the body (for example a bottom balance). See if they can make a long, low shape and a small, tucked shape as well as others (such as twisted).

Ask them to practise travelling into a new space to make this shape (for example side rolling to front support; bunny jump and sit back to bottom balance). After holding the shape for a count of three, ask them to lower their bodies down to the floor to roll or slide away. Repeat several times trying different combinations.

In pairs, ask the children to label themselves 'A' and 'B'. Ask the 'A's to balance and the 'B's to move around their partners (hopping, bunny jumping, rolling and so on). Can they balance so that their partners can move underneath? Tell them to try several ways, taking turns to do so.

Move on to ask the 'A's to make a low shape and the 'B's to jump over it. Again, make sure the children take turns to do this, without touching. Then see if they can jump over using a matching shape (for example a long thin balance – long thin jump; tucked shape – tucked jump). Move around, watching as they practise several variations of this.

Then ask them: *Can you do this making a contrasting shape?* This could be a star or tucked.

See if the 'A's can add a travelling action before they make their balance and if the 'B's can make a travelling action before and after their jump (such as cart-wheel and jump, hop and jump roll and jump). Tell them to change roles so that they both practise these actions.

Ask the pairs to choose different shapes to try and to see if they can select other actions to go over or under the still shapes.

12 mins Apparatus work
Remind the class how to get out the apparatus and where to position it in their pairs (each pair responsible for getting out or helping with their items).

Ask the children to explore and practise individually:
● jumping off their apparatus
● balancing on, against or beside their apparatus in different ways.

Ask the pairs to think about and try ways in which they could:

Diagram 12

● help their partners to land as they jump from the apparatus (off a bench, plank or box-top) – see if they can try several ways of doing this safely
● explore and try out ways of jumping over a partner (using just a mat, using a bench, using a box top or trestle table and mat)
● take it in turns for one of them to balance against or on the apparatus while their partner moves around or under them.

Ask them to try to link some of these actions together.

4 mins Cool-down
With partners (preferably of similar weight and height), ask the children to stand one behind the other. Explain that one of them is to take responsibility for taking his or her partner's weight. Ask them to stand with one foot in front of the other to make a firm, wide base and to place their flat hands on the shoulders of their partners (see Diagram 12).

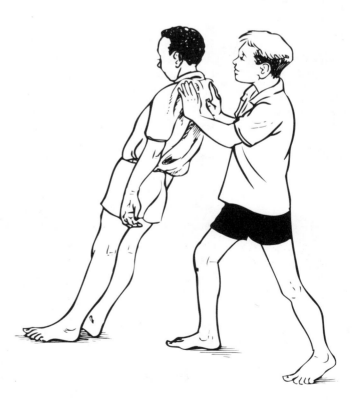

The other partner holds his body tense and firm and straight (it is important not to bend in the middle) and leans back to feel the strength of his partner's support. See if the children can trust their partners to take their weight, leaning back a bit more each time. Ask them to change over so all the children have an opportunity to take responsibility for their partners.

Finish by asking everyone to find a space and shake, stretch and relax.

Classroom review
Ask the children to talk about their sequences on the floor and on the apparatus and to try to record their best ideas so that they can practise and improve them next time.

Assessing learning outcomes
Are the children able to clarify their actions? How well are they working with their partners?

(40 mins) Can we move over our partners while they are moving?

Learning objectives
• Practise and refine jumps and balances, individually and in pairs.
• Explore ways of jumping and moving over a partner – as both a still and a moving obstacle.
• Explore and practise contrasting and matching shapes with a partner.
• Introduce assisted flight.
• Select and practise ways of moving over or under a partner on the apparatus.

Lesson organisation
Brief classroom discussion; warm-up individually and in pairs; floor work and apparatus work in pairs; paired and individual cool-down; teacher-led classroom review.

What you need and preparation
Organise apparatus for partner work. Before going to the hall, discuss with the class the particular requirements for partner work in gymnastics.

What to do

(6 mins) Warm-up
Individually, ask the class to skip all around the space using different directions, lifting their knees and pointing their toes to the ground.

In pairs, ask them to synchronise their steps. Ask them to choose their positions (such as side by side or one behind the other). Which foot do they start with? Ensure that they take turns to be leader.

Let the children practise and refine some of their favourite jumps on their own. Can they remember the different ways to take off (from one foot or two)? Can they

remember the different ways to land (onto one foot or two)? Use some demonstrations to illustrate a variety of possibilities and encourage them all to practise three different ways. Can they try them together? Ask them to show and then practise two special jumps in their pairs. Can they copy them exactly? Can they jump at the same time? Particularly ask them to practise a straddle jump (legs wide, keeping head up) and stretching in twos sitting back to back.

(18 mins) Floor work
Ask the pairs to select and practise some of their other favourite gymnastic moves, specifically balancing and ways of rolling. Encourage them by asking: *Can you make the shape very clear? How could you refine your moves?* Ask them to select two of each to practise with their partner.

**Partner work:
linking actions**

In pairs, ask them to try a balance which their partner can move around or under. Practise several ways, taking it in turns to make the balance. Then ask if they can try a balance which their partner can move over.

In pairs, ask them to try a roll, moving slowly, that their partner could move over. For example, one rolls and one jumps over using a matching shape (moving obstacle) such as: long, thin side roll – turning, thin jump; forward or side tucked roll – tucked jump. Can they try a contrasting shape? Are they contrasting or matching shapes?

Ask them to try ways of travelling over their partner other than jumping (for example cart-wheeling, bunny jumping, sliding).

Introduce the idea of assisted flight by asking pairs to take it in turns to help their partners to jump upwards. Suggest that they try supporting their partners by holding them under the elbows (see Diagram 13).

How many other ways can they find to do this? For example, standing one behind the other, one child uses the shoulders of her partner to press down on to help the jumping action. Encourage the children to support their partners to enable them to jump higher than they could do alone, or to stay in the air longer. Then ask them to clarify the shapes of their jumps.

Diagram 13

⏱ 12 mins Apparatus work

Tell the class to get out the apparatus, in pairs or fours where necessary.

Ask them to begin on their own by practising jumps in different ways and from different parts of their apparatus (benches, planks, low trestle tables). They could try this on different pieces of apparatus from last week.

Ask them to discuss and try ways they can help a partner to jump using the apparatus. Encourage them to try:
- moving onto the apparatus
- helping their partner, who takes off from the apparatus, to land on the mat or back on the apparatus. Where do they need to stand? What do they need to remember? (Supporter starts with legs apart so they can move back easily – see Diagram 14.)

Vocabulary
synchronise steps
straddle jump
contrasting
matching
balance
roll
jump
assisted flight

Diagram 14

CHAPTER 2
GYMNASTICS

Partner work:
linking actions

Ask the children to take turns to practise ways of balancing while their partners jump over and/or move under their shapes.

Can they select and practise two or three of their favourite ways which they could include in a sequence next week? Ask them to try these in a different order to see if they can join them together more smoothly or continuously. For example, one balancing, one going over or under, then that person balances and their partner goes over or under that shape in a different way.

④ Cool-down
mins With a partner (ideally of similar weight and height), remind them of the 'trust fall'. (One partner takes responsibility for taking the other's weight.) Remind the children supporting to stand with one foot in front of the other to make a firm, wide base and to place their flat hands on the shoulders of their partners who lean back to feel the strength of the support. Invite them to practise taking their partners' weight, the partner leaning back a bit more each time. Change over, so both partners have an opportunity to take responsibility for the other.

Then ask all the children to shake, stretch and relax.

Classroom review
Ask the pairs to think carefully about their ideas and to select and plan which apparatus they want to use for the next few weeks.

Assessing learning outcomes
Are the children looking after their partners as they jump? Are they beginning to refine their ideas?

⑪ Can we help a partner to jump?

Learning objectives
● Practise ways of leaping and jumping individually and in pairs, assisting partner's flight.
● Introduce and practise the leap-frog action.
● Practise floor sequences in pairs, taking responsibility for each other.
● Explore ways of linking actions.

Lesson organisation
Brief discussion in the classroom; exercises individually and in pairs; teacher-led classroom review.

What you need and preparation
You will need apparatus for partner work. Discuss with the class the special considerations for partner work.

What to do
⑪ Warm up
mins Ask the class to practise running in all directions around the hall and then to practise running and leaping. Encourage them to try using both legs to lead the action.

Then tell them to practise several different jumps, particularly the star jump and the straddle jump. Emphasise stretching their legs wide in the air but bringing them back together again for the landing. Ask them to practise some other ways of jumping, thinking about the shape they are making. Can they try the stag leap (see Diagram 15)? Can they think of other shapes in the air that they could try?

Ask them to perform a shoulder stretch in pairs. Explain that one of the pair sits on the floor and brings her arms up behind her. Her partner holds on to her arms and very gently tries to cross them. Tell them to hold this stretch for eight seconds and then relax. Ensure that they take it in turns.

Diagram 15

56

PRIMARY FOUNDATIONS: Physical education Ages 9–11

Floor work

18 mins Ask the children individually to practise some of their balances then some ways of travelling on their hands and feet.

Ask them to think of and practise some different ways of jumping with their partners. Encourage a variety of ideas and select some for demonstration for others to try.

Select a pair and ask them to demonstrate or teach a leap-frog action.

Ask the others to say what they think is important about making the base. (Stability, height.) Emphasise the need for stability (feet apart for a wide base) and ask the children to practise in pairs. Ensure that they take it in turns to jump and to be the base. Emphasise keeping their heads up as they jump, and encourage them, when they are the base, to try:

- with their hands on the floor
- with their hands on their ankles
- with their hands on their knees.

(See Diagram 16.)

Diagram 16

Then ask the children to try leaping and running and jumping (only a few steps). Ask them to think about:

Diagram 17

- How many steps do you take before you take off?
- How can you support your partners when they are moving?
- What do you need to do? (Move with them.)

Ask them to try other ways of moving over their partners. For example, one child kneels down to make a firm base on all fours and her partner bunny jumps sideways (see Diagram 17). Suggest they try this resting on their hands, then resting on their forearms.

Partner work: linking actions

Can they do this in another way? For example, they might perform a scissors action or cart-wheeling action over their partner. Ensure that they take it in turns to be the base. Ask them to remember and practise ways of working with a partner to combine in their sequence.

● Which one will they start with?
● Can they join them together more smoothly?
● Which travelling actions will they choose to help them get into position for the next move?

Apparatus work
12 mins

Ask the children to get out their allocated low apparatus.

Ask them to practise and refine some of their ways of balancing individually and then to practise moving under or over their partners.

Encourage them to try a leap-frog or other ideas using the apparatus. For example, one person makes a shape next to or over a bench and his partner jumps from this apparatus over his back (see Diagram 18).

Emphasise the need to for the jumper to keep his or her head up.

Ask the children to select and practise ways of linking some of their partner actions around on or over their apparatus.

Cool-down
4 mins

Ask the pairs to practise a shoulder stand and to take it in turns to match their partners' shapes.

Then tell everyone to stay in their shapes and lower their legs until they are in a lying position, then stretch and relax.

Classroom review

Ask the pairs to review their choices for their floor sequences. Which have they chosen? How do they want to start the sequence? Have they included some flight and some balance actions?

Assessing learning outcomes

Are the children refining their jumps? Are they able to support their partners? Are they all being careful?

Diagram 18

(40 mins) Can we balance with our partners?

What you need and preparation

You will need low apparatus for partner work; copies of photocopiable page 136.

Discuss with the class the special arrangements for doing gymnastics and the ways in which they are taking care of their partner. Introduce counterbalance – pulling or leaning away from a partner using a common or small base. Tell them that they will need to consider the base, the angle of leaning and the point of contact.

What to do

(5 mins) Warm-up

Ask the children to jog and then side-step around the space going in both directions. In pairs, see if they can face their partners and side-step in time with each other.

Ask them to practise turning jumps individually, taking off with two feet and landing on two feet, and then taking off with one foot and landing on the other, swinging their legs in the air as if they were crossing a line on the floor or high-jump bar.

Tell them to practise a shoulder stretch with their partners. The 'A's sit down with their arms above their heads, thumbs linked. 'B's stand behind them and very gently pull their arms back a little way. Tell them to hold this stretch for five seconds and then change over.

In pairs, ask them to practise different ways of assisting their partners to jump.

Diagram 19

(20 mins) Floor work

Ask the children to try this turning jump in pairs. Ask: *Can you think of different ways you can support your partner?* Encourage them to try or teach them the following:

● supporting your partner under her elbows with her leaning on your arms in order to kick her legs higher (see Diagram 19).

● with supporting hands together, assisting the lift and enabling your partner to stay in the air longer.

Now introduce counterbalance by asking the children to stand facing a partner with toes about 30cm apart. Holding both their partner's elbows firmly (forearms touching), ask them to lean away from each other to straighten the arms, keeping the body straight and firm. Stress that it is important not to sag or bend in the middle. (See Diagram 20.) Ask them to take care and time to adjust to their partner's weight and insist that they move slowly and carefully into the balance and complete the move in a controlled way.

Ask them what might happen if one partner exerts a stronger force than the other. *What happens if the contact is broken?* Emphasise that the move is not completed when the balance is held, but when both partners are back in a stable position. Encourage

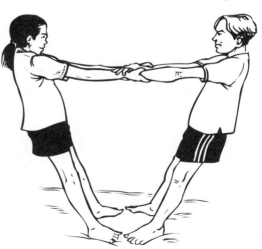

Diagram 20

Learning objectives
● Practise turning jumps, individually and with a partner.
● Introduce counterbalance.
● Work collaboratively with, and trust, a partner.
● Practise floor sequences in pairs.

Lesson organisation
Classroom introduction and discussion; warm-up individually and in pairs; floor and apparatus work in pairs; paired cool-down; teacher-led classroom review.

Partner work:
linking actions

Vocabulary
side-step
counterbalance
assisted flight

them to hold the balance for a count of three. Then ask them both to pull back to a standing position, and/or to bend their knees and lower themselves to sitting before releasing their grip. See if they can try this again getting their feet a bit closer to their partner to start with. See if they can try with toes touching or with their feet between each other.

See if the children can try any other ways of holding their partners to do this (for example holding wrists or hands or using one hand). Can they try different starting positions (such as sitting, kneeling, sideways)? Can they make some different shapes? Can they try some of the ways on photocopiable page 136?

Ask them to practise ways in which they could complete the move (for example returning to the original position or lowering each other or just one person to the ground). *Can you think of other ways of getting out of this balance?* (Stepping back onto one foot or lowering their partners to a sitting position, perhaps to roll backwards.)

Ask them to think of ways that they could travel to move away from their partners. Can they travel to balance in a space away from their partners?

Encourage them to help each other to practise, refine and perform floor sequences in pairs.

12 mins Apparatus work
Ask the children to practise some of the ways of jumping, with a partner assisting their flight or jumping over them.

Ask them to take it in turns to balance for their partner to move over or under them.

Then tell them to try some of the counterbalance ideas on the apparatus. For example, one sitting and one standing on a bench, leaning away from each other (see Diagram 21).

Diagram 21

3 mins Cool-down
In pairs, ask the children to practise a shoulder stand, this time making contrasting shapes with their legs. Tell them to lower their legs, lie still and relax.

Classroom review
Ask the children what they had to do to balance their partners. Talk about the base and the different angles of lean, adjusting to their partner's weight.

Assessing learning outcomes
Do the children trust and support each other? Can they lean against their partners to balance?

40 mins Can we lean or push against our partners to balance?

What you need and preparation

Organise apparatus for partner work.

Discuss with the class the special arrangements for doing partner work in gymnastics. Explain the difference between pulling away from each other (counterbalance or tension) and pushing towards or leaning against each other (counter resistance). Tell the children they will need to consider grip, point of contact and base.

What to do

4 mins Warm-up

Ask the children to jog and jump around the space in different directions. Then, with partners, ask them to take it in turns to be the leader, jogging and jumping with their partner following. When the leader stops to make a shape, their partner moves over them to take over the lead. Repeat several times using different shapes.

Ask them to practise and refine selected ways of assisting their partner to jump.

18 mins Floor work

Ask the children to remain in pairs to practise ways of moving over their partners. Remind them of the need to make a very stable base. Suggest they try a bunny jump over their partner who is kneeling on all fours on the floor. Can they lie across their partner in this position, lower their hands to the floor to move into a forward roll? Remind them to think about linking actions.

Diagram 22

When their partner has rolled over their base, what do they do next?

Now tell the pairs to practise their ideas for counterbalance with their partner. Particularly encourage them to practise ways of moving out of these balances.

Instead of pulling away from their partners, ask them to try some different ways of pushing, propping up or leaning against their partners, like the trust fall. For example, sitting back to back, ask them to link elbows and to bend their knees, putting their feet flatly and firmly on the ground with their heels close to their bottoms. Tell the children to push their backs hard against their partners' backs and to push their feet hard into the ground. (See Diagram 22.) See if they can stand up like this. Encourage them

CHAPTER 2
GYMNASTICS

**Partner work:
linking actions**

Vocabulary
counter resistance
lean
push
balance
linking
starting position
finishing position

by asking: *Can you do this without linking your elbows? Can you think of some other ways you can push against your partner to balance?*

Ask them to practise their partner floor sequences, thinking and discussing how they might improve the linking actions. Give them time to practise their ideas and observe another pair's sequence. Ask them:

● Is the end of one movement the start of the next?
● How can you get into the next position for your balance or flight with a partner?
Emphasise good starting and finishing positions.

Select examples to demonstrate a variety of positions and how these lead into the first move. Emphasise continuity and look for examples of smooth transitions between balance and flight actions. Select examples to demonstrate contrasting or matching shapes.

(15 mins) Apparatus work
Ask the pairs to remember and practise some of their favourite moves going under or over their partner, using some parts of the apparatus. Before they begin their sequence, ask them:

● Where will you start your sequence?
● Will you start by travelling towards the apparatus together or from different places?
● How will you finish your sequence? Will the finish be a controlled balance or will it be a dynamic jump?

Ask the pairs to select at least two of their balances and two assisted-flight actions to incorporate in a sequence. Encourage them to practise a sequence in pairs on the apparatus. How can they join their actions together smoothly?

(3 mins) Cool-down
In pairs, ask the children to hold hands and to pull away from their partners to lower to the ground, stretch out and relax.

Classroom review
Ask the children what they enjoyed most about the partner work. What could they do together that they could not do on their own? How did their partner help them?

Assessing learning outcomes
Are the children thinking carefully about their starting and finishing positions? How are they working together?

(40 mins) How can we improve our paired sequences?

Learning objectives
● Perform floor sequences in pairs.
● Refine a sequence in pairs on the apparatus.
● Comment and evaluate own work with a partner.
● Appreciate and acknowledge the work of others.

What you need and preparation
You will need apparatus for partner work.

Discuss the special considerations for doing partner gymnastics. Ask the pairs to remind themselves of some of the partner actions they will include in their sequences.

What to do
(6 mins) Warm-up
Ask the children to skip around the space in different directions, then ask them to practise some of the ways of assisting their partners' jumps, for example leap-frog and assisted flight.

Partner work: linking actions

⑩ Floor work

Ask the pairs to practise different ways of balancing with their partner, particularly trying to refine the counter resistance ideas (pushing, leaning against a partner). Have they included counterbalance and counter tension actions in their sequences? Which travelling actions are they going to use to link these moves?

Ask the children to practise, refine and perform their floor sequences in pairs.

Invite half the class to show the other half their sequences. Ask the group watching to pick out some smooth, linking movements and to say what they liked about them. *How did they contribute to the continuity of the sequence?*

⑳ Apparatus work

Ask the pairs to remember and practise some of their favourite moves going under or over their partner, using parts of the apparatus.

Ask the pairs to select at least two of their balances and two assisted-flight actions to incorporate into their sequence. Encourage them to practise a sequence in pairs on the apparatus. *How can you join your actions together smoothly?*

Ask them where they will start their sequence. Will they start together or from different places? Tell them to think about the finish – a balance or a dynamic jump.

Now tell them to watch and help another pair to refine their actions. What did they like? Which parts can be more smoothly joined?

Then ask everyone to refine and perform a sequence in pairs on the apparatus, taking into account any comments that others have made.

④ Cool-down

Ask the pairs to sit back to back and to stand up, pushing against their partners' backs. Can they lower themselves again?

Ask them to shake, stretch and relax, taking lots of deep breaths and acknowledging themselves for the effort they have put into practising and refining their sequences with their partners.

Classroom review

Ask the children to acknowledge and thank their partners.

Assessing learning outcomes

Were the children able to compose and practise their sequences on the floor and on the apparatus? Were they able to link the actions together smoothly?

Lesson organisation
Classroom discussion and revision; warm-up individually and in pairs; floor and apparatus work in pairs; cool-down in pairs; teacher-led classroom review.

Vocabulary
leap-frog
assisted flight
counter resistance
sequences
continuity

CHAPTER 3

Games

Many of the children in Years 5 and 6 should have developed a range of games skills around invasion, striking and fielding and net and wall activities. In the early stages of their games experience, much work will be confined to individual skills with a variety of equipment, but later on, these skills will be put into mini-team games. When playing games, children in Years 5 and 6 should be thinking of ways of using their games skills to outwit the opposition using a variety of strategies and tactics. This may result in a team scoring a goal, making a run or winning a point in opposition territory. Many children will bring with them knowledge of rules that relate to key games. In some cases children will make up their own rules to their games as well as being able to work collaboratively with a colleague or colleagues.

It is important early on to assess the individual needs of all the children to see what stage of games development they have reached. In some cases, children might need to consolidate their own individual skills, play in small-side games or improve through differentiated tasks or use of equipment. There is a strong case to group children by ability when teaching games.

A selection of quick games for warming up is provided on photocopiable pages 137 and 138.

Over the net (tennis)
The focus of this unit of work will give children experience of handling different types of rackets and balls in a variety of ways and help them acquire all the necessary skills which will allow them to play different forms of tennis activities.

Over the net (volleyball)
This unit will teach children the fundamental aspects involved in volleyball, namely volleying, digging and serving.

Invasion (rugby)
The focus of this unit of work is on the attacking, defending, passing and intercepting skills necessary for rugby.

Invasion (basketball)
The focus of this unit is on the attacking, defending, passing and intercepting skills necessary for basketball.

Striking and fielding
This unit focuses on batting, bowling and fielding, allowing children to acquire all the necessary skills to play cricket.

Some detailed notes on fielding skills are offered on photocopiable page 139.

Over the net (tennis)

This unit is divided into three sessions allowing 30–40 minutes of activity. All the work should be taught in the playground. It is important that every child has a short-headed racket and a small sponge ball to use during the individual activities section. The use of a foam ball will give children more time to strike.

During learning the children can:

- work individually or with a partner
- make up their own over the net activities using different rules
- find out why rules are important when playing a game
- be actively involved in their own learning
- achieve success in a purposeful and enjoyable way.

Children will need time to repeat, practise and consolidate their skills in order to build up their confidence and competence.

It is important that all children are given the opportunity to explore a range of striking equipment (padded bats, tennis rackets, squash rackets, table tennis bats, rounders bats and different-sized balls).

Enquiry questions	Learning objectives	Teaching activities	Learning outcomes
Can we improve our racket and ball skills?	● Introduce a variety of individual racket and ball skills with some paired activities. ● Practise moving, stopping and pivoting in different directions. ● Emphasise good footwork.	Warm-up: bouncing and catching a ball; jogging and then running around the space, touching the ground and moving on. Development: balancing a small ball on a racket and tapping it in the air; pushing the ball into the ground with a racket; hitting the ball continuously in the air; striking the ball against a wall; hitting the ball into targets. Games: bouncing and returning a ball; hitting a ball over a line continuously to each other. Cool-down: running around the space, then jogging, then walking.	Children: ● control the ball in different activities ● work co-operatively
What is a rally?	● Concentrate on partner and group activities using the individual striking skills learned. ● Apply the core skill of rallying into a mini-side game.	Warm-up: playing 'Follow my leader', alternately walking, running and jogging; in pairs, one following as other chassés sideways; throwing and catching in pairs. Games: hitting a ball continuously across a net in groups of six; playing rally games; keeping a ball going over a net for as long as possible. Cool-down: jogging around the space, balancing a ball on a racket, gradually slowing down to a walk.	● gain a greater sense of racket and ball control ● improve their footwork
Can we use our skills in a tennis-style game?	● Create and play a tennis-style game. ● Invent tennis games. ● Play mini-side competitive games.	Warm-up: playing a relay game in fours. Games: making up and playing a tennis game in fours; three versus one volleying activities. Cool-down: bouncing a ball on a racket.	● are creative and inventive in making up their own games ● use the skills previously learned in their games ● volley a ball with control and accuracy.

Cross-curricular links
Maths: using mathematical vocabulary involving counting, shapes and angles.

Resources
Bats; tennis rackets; squash rackets; table tennis bats; rounders bats; different-sized balls; hoops; cones; nets; ropes; photocopiable pages 137 and 138.

Over the net (tennis)

30 mins Can we improve our racket and ball skills?

Learning objectives
● Introduce a variety of individual racket and ball skills with some paired activities.
● Practise moving, stopping and pivoting in different directions.
● Emphasise good footwork.

Lesson organisation
Classroom introduction; individual warm-up and development; paired games; individual cool-down; teacher-led classroom review.

Vocabulary
serving
striking
rhythm
footwork
length
speed
height
rally
forehand
volley

What you need and preparation

You will need: a variety of different size bats and rackets; tennis balls; hoops.

Discuss in the classroom where the children are to go in the playground. Use the markings of a netball court (if you have one) as your teaching area. If not, mark out your area with cones or other markers.

What to do

5 mins Warm-up
Ask the children to *walk* anywhere in the working area, bouncing and catching a ball until told to stop.

Ask them to *jog* anywhere until told to stop, and on the command *Stop*, to touch the ground and then move on.

Now ask them to *run* anywhere until told to stop, and on the command *Stop*, to touch the ground and move on.

Encourage the children to take a large step when stopping in order to achieve a controlled

balance. Ask them why they need to make a wide base when they stop. To make it more difficult, make the running area smaller.

10 mins Development
With a suitable racket and ball each, ask the class to perform the following activities individually:
● Move around the playground balancing the ball on their racket – limit the space to make it more difficult if appropriate.
● Tap the ball gently into the air to bounce on the ground and then hit it again.
● Push the ball into the ground and then hit it again.
● Hit the ball continuously into the air, counting how many hits without the ball touching the ground they can achieve for their personal record.
● Move around the playground bouncing the ball on the racket.
● Strike the ball against a wall, let it bounce and then strike it again. (If there is no wall, ask them to pat the ball in the air, let it bounce and then hit it again.)
● Strike the ball against a wall, let it bounce into a hoop and then strike it again. (Or ask them to pat the ball in the air, let it bounce in a hoop and then strike it again – the hoop shape could be marked with chalk on the playground.)
● Strike the ball against a wall without letting it bounce, counting how many times they can hit the ball without it bouncing.
● Hit the ball into a variety of different-sized targets such as boxes or hoops.

10 mins Games
Ask the children to get into pairs, with one racket and one ball between two. Ask one child from each pair to bounce the ball to his or her partner, who must strike it back with the racket, for the sender to catch. Encourage the person who is bouncing the ball to be accurate in throwing. Ensure fair turns at bouncing and striking.

Ask the children to get one racket each, and to stand either side of a line, about three metres apart. Encourage them to hit the ball over the line to one another with one bounce.

Ask the pairs to move around the playground, bouncing the ball alternately to one another. How many continuous hits can each pair make?

⑤ Cool-down
Ask the children to run gently around the playground, followed by jogging and then walking.

Classroom review
Ask the children what they were successful at. Ask them what areas they need to improve on.

Assessing learning outcomes
Can the children control the ball in the different activities? Does each pair work co-operatively?

㉚ What is a rally?

What you need and preparation
You will need: rackets; tennis balls; nets; ropes; cones.

In the classroom, discuss with the children the previous lesson's work and what is going to be taught in this lesson. Make sure that the children are organised into pairs by ability. Draw a plan in the classroom of where each activity is to be played.

What to do
⑤ Warm-up
Ask the children to get into their pairs, and to play 'Follow my leader'. Explain that one partner is to alternately run, jog and walk about the space, and the other must shadow him or her as closely as possible, without touching.

Ask the pairs to label themselves 'A' and 'B' and to stand one behind the other, a little way apart. 'B' runs sideways (chassés) along a line and 'A' has to follow. After 45 seconds, tell the children to change roles.

Then ask the pairs to move around the playground, throwing a ball to each other, catching it either with or without a bounce.

⑳ Development and games
Ask the children to get into groups of six, and to lay out a rope on the ground. Ask three members of each group to stand in a line on one side of the rope, about two metres from it, and the other three members to stand in a line on the other side of the rope, again, about two metres from it. (Each player needs a racket, and there should be one ball per group.)

One player hits the ball over the rope to a player on the opposite side and then runs around a marker back to end of their line (see Diagram 1). The other player returns the ball to the next player facing and does the same. The object is to keep the rally going. The distance between the rope and the players can be made longer as the groups become more proficient. The ball may bounce once before being returned over the 'net'.

Still in groups of six, each with a racket, and one ball per group, and using the rope from the last game, ask five members

Learning objectives
● Concentrate on partner and group activities using the individual striking skills learned.
● Apply the core skill of rallying into a mini-side game.

Lesson organisation
Classroom discussion; paired warm-up; activities in small groups and pairs; individual cool-down; teacher-led classroom review.

Diagram 1

**Over the net
(tennis)**

Vocabulary
serving
striking
rhythm
footwork
length
speed
height
rally
forehand
volley

of each group to stand on one side of the rope, with the remaining player on the other side. The individual player must hit the ball alternately to the other five. Once the individual player has hit the ball, he must run around a marker and back to the middle to receive the next stroke. (See Diagram 2.) Once the first person in the group of five has hit the ball to the individual player, she goes to the back of their line. After the rally of five shots, ask the children to swap over to ensure that all players have a go at being the individual player. For example, the first person in the group of five becomes the individual player and the individual player goes to the back of the line of five.

Diagram 2

Position the marker nearer or further away from the individual player's starting position to make the game easier or more difficult.

Ask the children to return to their pairs, and to hit a ball over either a rope or a net to each other to see how long they can keep a rally going. In the first instance the ball can bounce twice before the ball is returned, eventually leading to one bounce before striking.

(5 mins) Cool-down
Ask the children to jog around the playground, balancing a small sponge ball on a racket, gradually slowing to a walk.

Classroom review
Discuss with the children how successful they were in their paired activities. Ask which group kept the ball going over the rope the longest.

Assessing learning outcomes
Are the children gaining a greater sense of racket and ball control? Is their footwork improving?

(30 mins) Can we use our skills in a tennis-style game?

Learning objectives
● Create and play a tennis-style game.
● Play mini-side competitive games.
● Invent tennis games.

Lesson organisation
Classroom revision and discussion; small-team warm-up and games; individual cool-down; teacher-led classroom review.

What you need and preparation
You will need: rackets; tennis balls; nets or ropes.

Ensure there is sufficient equipment for each group, and that each group is based on ability. Draw a plan as to who is playing in each area.

In the classroom, review what has been taught during the previous weeks, and then discuss with the children the expectations for this lesson.

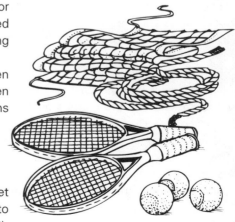

What to do
(5 mins) Warm-up
Ask the children to get into groups of four. Set up starting and finishing lines, and ask all the groups to stand in lines behind the starting line (see Diagram 3).

**Over the net
(tennis)**

Ask the first member of each group to hop to the finishing line and then to run back to the starting line, and then to 'tag' the next member of her group, who then does the same, and so on until everyone has done the exercise. Time how long it takes for the whole class to finish the activity.

20 mins **Development and games**
Ask the children to remain in groups of four, with two teams of two on either side of a net. Children must be given a clearly defined area to work in with all the equipment needed to play an over-the-net activity. Ask the groups to invent an over-the-net game of their own. Encourage them to answer the following questions to ensure a quality game:
● How does a rally start?
● How does each team score?
● How do you decide on the result?
● What height should the net be?
● How can the game be made easier or harder? (For example, to make it easier, allow more bounces when returning the ball, or only volley type returns are allowed to make it harder.)

Once they have mastered their game, ask the groups to play some competitive volleying. One player hits the ball over the net and the other team has to return the ball without it bouncing. Encourage each team to see how many volleys they can make in 15, 30, 45 and 60 seconds.

In their teams of four on one court, ask the children to stand in lines to play a different volleying game. The game starts with one person hitting the ball over an improvised net. The ball must be returned without it bouncing on the floor. After each person has hit the ball, she returns to the back of the line. Ask the children to keep rotating until the ball either touches the ground or goes out of court.

5 mins **Cool-down**
Ask the children individually to bounce the ball on a racket without it dropping to the ground.

Classroom review
Ask the children how the tennis activities went with those groups that made up their own games. Were they successful? How could the game be improved? Were all the children successful in volleying a ball or do they need more practice?

Assessing learning outcomes
How creative and inventive are the children in making up their own games? Do they use the skills previously learned in their games? In the competitive games, are all the children able to volley a ball with control and accuracy?

> **Diagram 3**
>
> ———————————————— finishing line
>
>
>
> ———————————————— starting line

Vocabulary
serving
striking
rhythm
footwork
length
speed
height
rally
singles
forehand
volley
doubles
court
score

Over the net (volleyball)

The focus of this unit of work is to allow children to be introduced to a no-bounce game that uses just hands.

The unit of work is divided into three sessions allowing 30–40 minutes of activity per session. Skills can be taught indoors (preferably in a large or medium-sized hall) and also in the playground. For practice a large (size 3 or 4), light, soft ball must be used. Some foam balls are ideal at the beginning stages. A net can be set up using a long rope that runs the length of the hall. This should be about 2 to 2.5 metres high to encourage passing the ball up and over. Bands can be attached to the rope to divide the net into smaller playing areas.

It is assumed that the children have experienced catching and throwing activities using large balls.

Enquiry questions	Learning objectives	Teaching activities	Learning outcomes
How do we volley a volleyball?	● Practise catching and throwing games over a net. ● Vary the height of the net in order to develop confidence and success.	Warm-up: playing 'Catch the tail' in pairs. Development: individually practising throwing and catching; volleying with two hands; volleying in pairs. Game: throwing and catching the ball, throwing for a partner to volley, then digging to return; keeping the ball up. Cool-down: volleying a ball individually, then passing it around the body.	Children: ● follow the path of the ball successfully in order to get underneath it (tracking) ● have the skills to volley and dig the ball ● co-operate in pairs to beat their record
How do we serve a volleyball?	● Practise volleying individually and in pairs. ● Practise digging. ● Introduce and practise the underam serve.	Warm-up: playing 'Tag release'. Development: practising throwing and catching individually, then volleying with two hands, keeping the ball above the head; volleying in pairs. Game: throwing and catching the ball, throwing for a partner to volley, then digging to return over the net; keeping the ball up. Cool-down: volleying a ball individually, then passing it around the body.	● improve their volleying action ● control their digging and serving
Can we improve our serving, volleying and digging actions?	● Practise and improve volleying individually and in pairs. ● Practise and improve digging. ● Practise the underam serve. ● Combine the skills of volleying, digging and serving in a game.	Warm-up: playing 'North, south, east, west', varying the actions. Development: practising digging in pairs; playing keep the ball up using different parts of the body; volleying over the net in pairs; digging in pairs. Game: playing keep it up; playing volleyball (two versus two). Cool-down: volleying and/or digging a ball individually, then passing it around the body.	● control the ball as they volley, dig and serve.

Cross-curricular links
Maths: using mathematical vocabulary involving shapes and angles.

Resources
Large, lightweight balls; nets (or ropes and poles); cones; chalk; photocopiable pages 137 and 138.

**Over the net
(volleyball)**

⓸⑤ mins How *do* we volley and dig a volleyball?

What you need and preparation
Ensure there are enough large balls for each child to use, which are lightweight and well inflated. A long rope between two posts can serve as a net. You will also need small bands.

In the classroom, ensure that the children understand where to go, and what the playing area is.

What to do

⑤ mins Warm-up
Ask the children to get into pairs, and to label themselves 'A' and 'B'. 'A' has a band tucked in the back of their shorts. 'B' has to try to pull the band from their partner's shorts without touching them. If 'B' gets the band the roles are reversed, with 'A' trying to retrieve the band from 'B'.

㉕ mins Development
Ask the children to get a lightweight volleyball each, and then to practise throwing and catching the ball with two hands, keeping it above their heads. Encourage them to keep their arms high, with elbows slightly bent, and to move their feet about shoulder-width apart to keep repositioning themselves to stay under the ball. Ask them if they can vary the height of the throw but still throw it upwards rather then forwards. Ask them to try to do this and touch the ball less and less. Emphasise doing so with both hands simultaneously. How long can they keep the ball up?

In pairs, with one ball between two, ask the children if they can do this with partners. *How many quick upward throws and catches can you make without the ball dropping?*

Introduce the volley. Ask the children to cushion the ball with fingers and thumbs spread and held above their heads so that the fingers and thumbs nearly make a circle that can be looked through (up towards the ceiling or watching the ball) – see Diagram 4.

Individually, ask them to tap the ball up in the air, using the soft tips of their fingers. Encourage keeping their feet slightly apart with one foot just in front of the other. Encourage them to volley the ball a little higher, using the legs as well as the arms. Ask: *How many times can you keep it up?* If the ball drops to the ground, encourage the children to throw it up into the air above them and to volley it again.

In pairs, ask the children to face each other about three metres apart. One child throws the ball into the air and volleys it up in the air for his or her partner to catch, just above the forehead. The partner then throws the ball up for the first sender to volley back. How many volleys can they make without the ball falling to the ground? Can they do this without catching the ball?

Introduce the dig by asking the children to place one hand on top of the other, with palms facing upwards. Tell them to press their thumbs down and away from the body to make a flat

Diagram 4

Learning objectives
● Practise catching and throwing games over a net.
● Vary the height of the net in order to develop confidence and success.

Lesson organisation
Classroom discussion; paired warm-up; individual and paired activities; individual cool-down; teacher-led classroom review.

Vocabulary
volleying
service
digging
spiking
jumping
tracking

**Over the net
(volleyball)**

platform to play the ball with a simultaneous touch of the wrists (see Diagram 5). Encourage them to practise the action in pairs, with the players tossing the ball gently upwards towards their partners for them to dig to return. Encourage them to bend their knees and to keep low, with their arms nearly horizontal as they play the ball (guiding it upwards). Encourage them to dig the ball upwards for their partners to catch, and ensure fair turns.

Diagram 5

10 mins **Games**
Ask the children to try volleying the ball upwards and over a net backwards and forwards to their partner. Advise them not to stand too far apart, and emphasise volleying the ball upwards. How long can they keep the rally going?

Encourage them to play 'Keep it up', using either volleying or digging. If the ball falls below shoulder height, encourage them to dig the ball up and then volley it.

5 mins **Cool-down**
Ask the children to volley the ball into the air as many times as possible without it dropping to the ground. Ask them to pass the ball around their bodies and between their legs. Then tell them to put the balls away and relax.

Classroom review
Ask the children if they are clear about the terminology of volleying and digging. Ask them what they found hard, or easy which will help to plan the next lesson.

Assessing learning outcomes
Can all the children follow the path of the ball successfully in order to get underneath it (tracking)? Do all the children have the skills to volley and dig the ball? Are they co-operating in pairs to beat their record?

40 mins How do we serve a volleyball?

Learning objectives
● Practise volleying individually and in pairs.
● Practise digging.
● Introduce and practise the underarm serve.

Lesson organisation
Classroom revision; whole-class warm-up; activities in pairs and individually; individual cool-down; teacher-led classroom review.

What you need and preparation
Ensure there are enough balls for all the children to use that are lightweight and well inflated. Set up a long net or rope to serve as a volleyball net.

In the classroom, discuss with the children what happened in the previous lesson in relation to the core skills of volleying and digging.

What to do
5 mins **Warm-up**
Ensure that all the children are well spaced out in a small area (for example one-third of a netball court). Choose one of the children to be the 'tagger'. This child has to tag the others, who must stay in the defined area. If a person is tagged then they have to stand still with their arms stretched outwards until someone runs under an arm, which releases them back into the game. If necessary, have more than one person tagging.

Over the net
(volleyball)

20 **Development**
mins Ask the children to get into pairs with one volleyball between two, and to practise volleying the ball, keeping it in the air, and taking it in turns to play the ball. Prompt them by asking: *How many volleys can you make before the ball falls to the ground? What do you need to remember?*

Then ask them to try this over the high net. If necessary, encourage them to volley the ball twice before returning it, to keep the ball in play (although this is not allowed in the rules of a volleyball game).

Still in pairs, ask the children to practise digging, with one player feeding their partner by tossing the ball up underarm for their partner to dig. Change over at frequent intervals. Encourage them to dig the ball up into the air for their partner to catch. Can they keep the ball up digging or volleying in pairs?

Introduce the underarm service. Ask the children to hold the ball out in front of them with the non-striking hand below waist height. Standing with the foot opposite the striking arm forward, ask them to strike the ball (like an underarm throw) over the net, ensuring that the thumb is against the forefinger, which allows the heel of the hand to hit the ball first (see Diagram 6). Encourage the children to practise this individually and then in pairs, asking the partners to collect the ball and serve to return it. Ensure a good follow-through using an underarm swing.

Diagram 6

10 **Games**
mins In pairs, ask one child to throw the ball up and then to volley it to their partner over the net. Encourage the players to keep the ball up, volleying or digging. When they have had some practice doing this, ask them to try to start the game with an underarm service. Rather than stand too far away from the net, advise them to stand where they can successfully get the ball over the net. It is important at this stage to keep the ball going.

Vocabulary
volleying
service
digging
spiking
jumping
underarm

5 **Cool-down**
mins Ask the children to dig the ball into the air as many times as possible without it dropping to the ground. Ask them to pass the ball around their bodies and between their legs. To finish, ask everyone to put the balls away and then relax.

Classroom review
Discuss with the children if they were successful in the underarm serving action, especially over the net. *How did you manage the digging and serving? What did you need to remember?*

Assessing learning outcomes
How are the children improving their volleying actions? Are they able to control their digging and serving?

**Over the net
(volleyball)**

50 mins Can we improve our serving, volleying and digging actions?

Learning objectives
• Practise and improve volleying individually and in pairs.
• Practise and improve digging.
• Practise the underarm serve.
• Combine the skills of volleying, digging and serving in a game.

Lesson organisation
Classroom discussion; whole-class warm-up; individual and paired development; paired and small-group games; individual cool-down; teacher-led classroom review.

Vocabulary
volleying
service
digging
spiking
jumping
blocking
smashing

What you need and preparation

You will need: balls; grids; nets or ropes suspended between poles; cones or chalk.

In the classroom, discuss how the serve was taught in the previous lesson.

What to do

5 mins **Warm-up**
Mark the playground or hall into four areas – north, south, east and west. Use an existing grid (for example the netball court) or cones, markers or chalk.

Ask the children to run around the space without touching each other, and tell them that on your signal (*North*, *South*, *East* or *West*), you want them to run to that area, without bumping into each other.

To vary the action, ask the children to hop around the space and, on your signal, run to the specified area.

20 mins **Development**
Ask the children to practise digging in pairs, with one player feeding their partner, then with both trying to keep the ball up. Emphasise using two hands.

Ask them to try to play 'Keep the ball up', using other parts of the body above the waist. How many parts can they use? How many taps can they make before the ball drops to the ground?

In pairs, with one volleyball between two, ask them to practise volleying the ball to each other over the high net. Encourage them to try to beat their record number of volleys.

Ask the pairs to practise digging, with one player feeding his or her partner by tossing the ball up underarm for the partner to dig. Encourage them to make simultaneous touches with their wrists. Remind them to change over at frequent intervals.

15 mins **Games**
In pairs, ask the children to play 'Keep it up'.

Then ask each pair to join another pair to play a two versus two game, and to see how many times they can keep the ball up passing to their partner and over the net. Encourage them to take it in turns to serve.

If they are doing well, they can be encouraged to compete against their partners. Using a well-defined area, they can score a point if the ball falls to the ground on their opponents' side of the net.

5 mins **Cool-down**
Ask the children to volley or dig the ball into the air as many times as possible without it dropping to the ground. Then tell them to pass the ball around their bodies and between their legs. To finish, ask them to put the balls away and then relax.

Classroom review

How may passes could the children make to their partners before the ball dropped? Ask them if they were able to pass to a partner before volleying or digging the ball over the net.

Assessing learning outcomes

Are the children controlling the ball as they volley, dig and serve?

Invasion (rugby)

The focus of this unit of work will allow children to experience handling different types of rugby balls through independent, partner and mini-side activities.

During this unit, the children will:

- improve their handling skills
- understand the importance of attacking and defending
- value the importance of teamwork
- improve their spatial awareness.

The unit is divided into three lessons allowing 30–40 minutes of activity per lesson. All work should be taught in the playground.

It is assumed that all the children have experience of catching and throwing of different types of rugby balls, have an understanding of spatial awareness and some knowledge of the tactics required for the game.

Enquiry questions	Learning objectives	Teaching activities	Learning outcomes
What are the key skills required for rugby?	● Become familiar with a variety of individual and partner skills. ● Practise dodging and moving quickly in different directions. ● Practise throwing, catching and picking up a rugby ball. ● Practise passing a rugby ball and introduce passing it backwards.	Warm-up: in pairs, trying to grab a band from each other, and dodging to avoid; whole-class trying the same. Development: catching and throwing a rugby ball; passing a rugby ball using both hands in pairs; carrying a rugby ball, weaving through obstacles and passing to a partner. Cool-down: throwing a rugby ball in the air, clapping before catching it.	Children: ● carry a ball with two hands ● pass a ball backwards ● feed the ball accurately in the air to catch it again ● catch a ball with good technique
Can we catch, pass, dodge and defend?	● Reinforce skills around catching, passing and dodging. ● Practise passing a rugby ball in a small team activity without it being intercepted. ● Play a small-side game of rugby with emphasis on attacking, defending and scoring.	Warm-up: five children each with a rugby ball trying to touch the others with the ball. Development: running with a ball, scoring and passing to another person in groups; small groups passing the ball to each other, trying to avoid interception; playing a small-side game involving attacking, defending and scoring a try. Cool-down: jogging and passing the ball backwards in groups of five.	● support a player when they were tagged in order to receive a pass
Can we combine our skills into a game of mini-rugby?	● Work on passing a rugby ball sideways and backwards using two hands. ● Playing mini-side rugby games involving attacking, defending and scoring a try. ● Encourage team members to support the ball carrier.	Warm-up: passing a rugby ball sideways in twos and threes. Development: playing a mini-side game involving attacking, defending and scoring; repeating the activity, but this time if the attacker is 'caught', the ball goes to the other team. Cool-down: jogging around the space passing the ball sideways and slightly backwards in pairs.	● pass sideways on the move ● stick to rules ● understand what tactics could be brought into the rugby games by the attackers and defenders to outwit the other team.

Cross-curricular links
PSHE: working alone and with others; agreeing rules; communication skills.
Science: gaining awarness of how the body works.
Maths: using mathematical vocabulary involving shapes and angles; an understanding of area.

Resources
Foam rugby balls (sizes 3 and 4); rugby balls (sizes 3 and 4); bands; cones; hoops; photocopiable pages 137 and 138.

Invasion
(rugby)

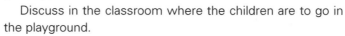

35 mins What are the key skills required for rugby?

Learning objectives
● Become familiar with a variety of individual and partner skills.
● Practise dodging and moving quickly in different directions.
● Practise throwing, catching and picking up a rugby ball.
● Practise passing a rugby ball and introduce passing it backwards.

Lesson organisation
Classroom introduction; paired and whole-class warm-up; individual, paired and small-group activities; individual cool-down; teacher-led classroom review.

Vocabulary
rules
passing
supporting
receiving
defending
attacking

What you need and preparation

Try to have rugby balls (enough for one each) appropriately placed in the playground before the lesson starts. If not, have the equipment ready to take into the working area. You will also need small bands and hoops. Mark the area you want the children to work in by using existing playground markings or cones.

Discuss in the classroom where the children are to go in the playground.

What to do

5 mins Warm-up

Ask the children to take a band each and to tuck it into the back of their shorts.

In pairs, ask the children to label themselves 'A' and 'B'. Explain that you want the 'A's to try to take the bands from the 'B's as many times as possible in 30 seconds. Once 'A' has caught the band, it is given back to 'B' to start the game again. It is important to stress no physical contact.

Once this has been mastered, 'A' and 'B' can try to get each other's band as well as defend their own. Restrict the area in the playground for this activity by making up small zones using markers.

Turn the activity into a whole-class activity, encouraging the children to see how many bands they can collect while defending their own. Play the game for 30 seconds. The winner is the person who collects the most bands. When playing the game, children must ensure there is enough of the band hanging from the back of their shorts for the others to grab. Let the children know that they must not hold onto their band when chasing or defending.

15 mins Development

Ask the children to get a rugby ball, and to stand in a space, throwing it into the air and catching it. Encourage them to make a cradle with their arms for the ball to fall into, and once the ball is caught, to hug it to the chest.

Ask them to move around the playground throwing and catching the rugby ball.

In a space, ask the children to roll the rugby ball away, chase after it and pick it up with two hands. Remind them to think about where they are going and to avoid bumping into other people.

Organise the children into pairs and tell them to face one another with a gap of eight metres between them. Ask them to roll the ball to one another. Encourage them to watch the ball, gather it up and then roll it back to their partners.

Then ask the pairs to move a little closer to each other, and to pass the rugby ball to each other, always using two hands to catch and release the ball.

Ask the pairs to position themselves two metres apart and then jog around the playground, passing the rugby ball to each other either forwards or sideways. Then ask them to repeat the action, but this time passing the ball backwards to each other.

10 mins Games

Organise the children into groups of six, and then split those groups into two teams of three. One group of three will be Team A, the other Team B. Ask the groups to take two hoops

and four cones, and to lay the hoop on the ground with the four cones leading away from it and towards the other hoop (see Diagram 7).

Diagram 7

Then ask them to place a rugby ball in the hoop. The first person in Team A picks up the rugby ball from their hoop with two hands and weaves in and out of the cones to place the rugby ball in Team B's hoop. The first person in Team B picks up the rugby ball and weaves in and out of the cones and places the ball back in Team A's hoop. The game carries on until everyone has picked up the ball, run with it and placed it in a hoop. Stress that the rugby ball must be carried with both hands. Place the cones closer together to make the weaving more difficult, or further apart to make it easier.

Put the hoops away, and ask the children to repeat the activity, but this time the rugby ball is *passed* to the first member of the other team. Advise that the pass should be aimed at around waist height.

Cool-down
5 mins Ask the children to throw the rugby ball in the air and see how many times they can clap their hands before catching it.

Classroom review
Ask the children why they think the ball should be held in two hands. Ask them why is it important to pass the ball at waist height.

Assessing learning outcomes
Do all the children carry the ball with two hands? Are they able to pass the ball backwards? Can they feed the ball accurately in the air to catch it again? Can they catch the ball with good technique?

30 mins Can we catch, pass, dodge and defend?

What you need and preparation
You will need: cones; rugby balls; hoops. Ensure that the equipment is appropriately placed in the playground or ready to collect on the way out. Have enough markers/cones to create small playing areas.

In the classroom, discuss with the children what was covered the previous week and where they are to go in the playground.

What to do
Warm-up
5 mins In the playground, mark out a large area with cones or use two-thirds of a netball court. Give five of the children a rugby ball each, and tell them to chase the others. Explain that, once touched by a rugby ball, a player must stand still with his or her arms outstretched. She can be released when another player runs under her arms. Nobody must go outside the playing area and the taggers must hold the rugby ball with both hands. The idea is to see how many children are standing still when 60 seconds has been reached. More or fewer taggers can be introduced to make the game harder or easier.

After 60 seconds, change the taggers and play the game again.

Learning objectives
- Reinforce skills around catching, passing and dodging.
- Practise passing a rugby ball in a small team activity without it being intercepted.
- Play a small-side game of rugby with the emphasis on attacking, defending and scoring.

Lesson organisation
Classroom discussion; whole-class warm-up; small-group activities; small-group cool-down; teacher-led classroom review.

Invasion (rugby)

Vocabulary
rules
passing
supporting
marking
receiving
defending
attacking
scoring
try
intercept

Development

20 mins

Organise the children into groups of five, with one rugby ball each. Ask them to lay out five cones, a metre apart from each other, leading up to a hoop, and then to get into a line behind the first cone.

The first person in the line holds their rugby ball in both hands and weaves in and out of the five cones placed in a line. At the end of the line of cones, the player puts the rugby ball into the hoop to indicate a try has been scored and runs back to his or her team. The second player goes and the game is completed when all the team have run in and out of the cones and all five rugby balls are in the hoop.

Still in groups of five, ask the children to play a four versus one game. One person should be nominated as the chaser, leaving the other four as passers. The passers must pass the ball to each other, never allowing it to go above head height, and count how many passes they can perform in 30 seconds. The chaser's job is to intercept the ball, and prevent a pass from being made.

Ask the children to stay in groups of five, for a game of five-a-side, working in a grid of 11 metres by 13 metres (see Diagram 8).

The idea is for each team to score in their opponents' try area. Explain that each team can run with the ball, but when tagged around the waist, a player must stop moving and should pass the rugby ball in any direction to a team-mate. If a team is tagged consecutively three times, the rugby ball goes to the other side. A try is scored by running with the ball into the opponents' try area, carrying it with both hands. The rugby ball must not be passed over head height. If this occurs, the ball goes to the other side.

Diagram 8	
try area A	1 metre
ꙮꙮ ꙮꙮ ꙮꙮ ꙮꙮ ꙮꙮ ꙮꙮ ꙮꙮ ꙮꙮ ꙮꙮ ꙮꙮ	11 metres
try area B	1 metre

Cool-down

5 mins

Ask the children to line up in fives, and jog and pass the ball backwards along the line.

Classroom review
Ask the children what effect the five-a-side rugby game had on their bodies. Were there any difficulties in passing the rugby ball backwards?

Assessing learning opportunities
Do team members support a player when they are tagged, in order to receive a pass?

Invasion
(rugby)

(30 mins) Can we combine our skills into a game of mini-rugby?

What you need and preparation
You will need: enough rugby balls for one between two. Mark out the area you want the children to work in by using existing playground markings or cones.

Discuss in the classroom where the children are to go in the playground for all the activities.

What to do

(5 mins) Warm-up
In pairs, ask the children to run lightly around the playground, passing the ball sideways to each other.

Now in threes, ask the children to run around the playground, passing the ball sideways to one another. After two complete sets of passes, the middle person changes position.

Now ask the threes to repeat the activity, but this time it is to be played in a grid with two try lines. When a member of the three crosses the try line, the ball is placed on the ground using two hands.

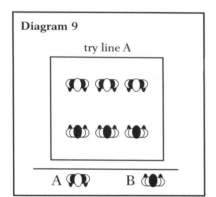

Diagram 9

(20 mins) Development
Ask the children to get into groups for three-a-side activities. Ask them to arrange themselves in a line each of defenders and attackers, facing each other (see Diagram 9 – A: defender, B: attacker).

Three attackers begin to pass the ball from the start line in an attempt to score in their opponents' try area. Explain that the ball has to be passed sideways. The three defenders must try to prevent the attackers from crossing their try line. If a defender touches the waist of an attacker with two hands when they have the ball in their hands, the attacker must stop immediately and pass the rugby ball sideways to one of their team members. The attacking team has two minutes to see how many tries they can score – then they change over to become defenders.

Now ask the children to play the game again, but this time both sides must try to both score and defend (see Diagram 10). If the ball goes forward or is dropped, possession goes to the other side. Encourage team members to support the ball carrier. All passes must go sideways. Divide the game into two halves, for example of four minutes each way.

(5 mins) Cool-down
In pairs, ask the children to jog around the playground, passing the ball sideways and slightly backwards.

Classroom review
Ask the children how many tries each team scored in their mini-side rugby games. Ask each team what strategies they used to attack and defend.

Assessing learning outcomes
Are the children able to pass sideways on the move? Do each team stick to the rules? What tactics could be brought into the rugby games by the attackers and defenders to outwit the other team?

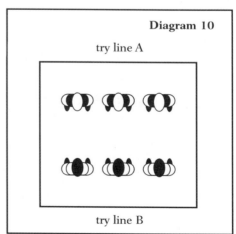

Diagram 10

Invasion (basketball)

The purpose of this unit is for children to improve their attacking and defending basketball skills through individual and partner work, leading to mini-side games. The children need to be aware of how to keep possession, defend their goal without the ball, work with the other members of their team and find ways of getting into a good position to shoot for goal.

This unit is divided into three sessions to allow 30–40 minutes of activity per session. All the work would be best taught in the playground, but can be adapted for a primary school hall. If proper fixed hoops are not available, any form of container will do (for example waste paper baskets, dustbins, plastic hoops, washing baskets). As in any planning, some of the activities from previous weeks may have to be repeated to consolidate learning.

Enquiry questions	Learning objectives	Teaching activities	Learning outcomes
How do we pass, receive, dribble and shoot a basketball?	● Improve dribbling, passing and receiving skills. ● Practise passing and intercepting in small-side activities. ● Practise moving with control with the ball.	Warm-up: dribbling a basketball around the space, emphasising pushing the ball firmly into the floor. Development: practising chest passes and moving into space to receive the ball; practising dribbling the ball in and out of a line of cones using alternate hands; playing a passing and intercepting game in small groups. Cool-down: dribbling around the space without looking at the ball.	Children: ● perform bounce passes and chest passes correctly ● improve their shooting skills ● are in control of their ball when dribbling
Can we improve our dribbling and shooting skills?	● Improve dribbling skills through close control. ● Improve defending skills through good footwork and ball awareness. ● Improve the accuracy of shooting.	Warm-up: walking around the space, dribbling a ball just below waist height. Development: practising dribbling and defending the ball whilst moving around the space; defending a skittle from being knocked over by three attackers; aiming accurately; incorporating all skills into a small-side game involving four versus four. Cool-down: practising chest and bounce passes.	● improve the accuracy of their shooting ● dribble and pass a ball with control and accuracy
What strategies can we use for attacking and defending?	● Develop more advanced passing and receiving skills. ● Use strategies to pass the basketball without it being intercepted. ● Find ways of outwitting an opponent to score as many points as possible.	Warm-up: playing a running activity in groups of seven in a fixed area. Development: playing mini-side games involving teams using passing strategies to avoid interception; playing another mini-side activity, trying to outwit opponents in order to score. Cool-down: practising dribbling around the space using alternate hands.	● move into space to receive a pass ● mark their opponents to prevent them receiving the ball.

Cross-curricular links
Science: being aware of how the body works and reacts to exercise.

Resources
Basketballs (various sizes); basketball hoops/rings; cones; skittles; photocopiable pages 137 and 138.

30 mins How do we pass, receive, dribble and shoot a basketball?

What you need and preparation
You will need basketballs (size 3/4); cones.

In the classroom, discuss the game of basketball with the children, what is expected from the lesson and the importance of good ball control skills.

What to do

5 mins Warm-up
Ask the children to run around the playground, and on a given signal change direction.

Ask them to run sideways along a line for six steps forwards and then backwards for six steps. Repeat this four times.

20 mins Development
Ask the children to dribble a basketball anywhere around the playground, emphasising the ball being pushed firmly to the floor.

Organise the children into pairs, and tell them to chest pass the ball to their partners. Once they have mastered this, ask them to pass the ball to their partners and then move quickly into another space – chest pass and move.

Now ask them to repeat the activity, but this time to bounce pass the ball to their partners.

Ask the pairs to combine into groups of four, and to lay out three cones placed one metre apart. The first member of the team dribbles in and out around the cones, and then runs back to the starting position and passes the ball to the next person. Encourage the children to try to dribble without looking at the ball, and encourage dribbling with left and right hands.

Repeat the activity, but this time, the first member of the team dribbles in and out of the cones and then bounces the ball on the ground past the last cone, then dribbles back to pass the ball to the next person in the team. The game is completed when all the team members have completed the exercise.

Ask the children to get into groups of five, and to nominate one member of their group to be the chaser. The remaining four members are to stand in a circle and pass the basketball to each other, but not to the person next to them (passes must be either chest passes or bounce passes across the circle). The chaser in the middle of the circle must try to intercept any passes. If the chaser intercepts the ball, the last person to pass the ball goes into the middle. Those in the circle are not allowed to move. If after ten passes the person in the middle has not intercepted the ball, someone else becomes the chaser.

5 mins Cool-down
On their own, ask the children to walk anywhere in the playground, dribbling the ball without looking at it.

Classroom review

Ask the class how the dribbling activity in and out of the cones could be made easier or harder. Can they describe one of the games they played?

Assessing learning outcomes

Are the bounce passes and chest passes correctly performed? How could the shooting skills be made harder for the next lesson? Are all the children in control of the ball when dribbling?

(30 mins) Can we improve our dribbling and shooting skills?

Learning objectives
- Improve dribbling skills through close control.
- Improve defending skills through good footwork and ball awareness.
- Improve the accuracy of shooting.

Lesson organisation
Classroom discussion; individual warm-up; group activities; paired cool-down; teacher-led classroom review.

Vocabulary
dribbling
shooting
marking
zones
chest pass
lay-up
shielding
attacking
defending
possession

What you need and preparation

You will need basketballs (size 3 or 4); hoops; skittles; basketball rings.

In the classroom, discuss with the children the dribbling activities covered the previous week and the key points for success.

What to do

(5 mins) Warm-up

Ask the children to walk around, bouncing the ball just below hip or waist height, on the same side as the hand they are using to dribble.

Play a number game. Ask the children to dribble the ball in and out, responding to the following commands:
- *One*: dribble and run.
- *Two*: bounce the ball on the spot without looking at it.
- *Three*: dribble the ball and walk.
- *Four*: bounce the ball in control whilst sitting on the floor.

(20 mins) Development

In a marked out grid, ask each child to dribble a ball. As the children move around, explain that they should try to knock away another person's ball but still keep in control of their own ball. There should be no physical contact.

Ask the children to get into groups of four, and to nominate one member of the group as the defender. A hoop is placed on the ground with a skittle in it. The defender must defend that skittle, but must not touch it or go in the hoop. The other three players move around the skittle, passing the ball to one another. The ball must be passed three times before the attackers aim to knock down the skittle. Discourage running with the ball. The defenders can defend their skittle using any part of the body. Once the attackers have scored three points, a new defender takes over.

In pairs, ask the children to practise shooting into a variety of target baskets laid out in the playground – two teams to a basket. One team watches while the other performs, then change over. Each team has two minutes to see how many baskets they can score. Ensure there is a clear shooting line to aim from. If there are not enough basketball rings, use circles on the wall or on the playground. The team watching keeps the score, the time, and returns the balls to the throwers. Emphasise a two-handed overhead release when shooting for the basket.

(30 mins) How do we pass, receive, dribble and shoot a basketball?

What you need and preparation

You will need basketballs (size 3/4); cones.

In the classroom, discuss the game of basketball with the children, what is expected from the lesson and the importance of good ball control skills.

What to do

(5 mins) Warm-up

Ask the children to run around the playground, and on a given signal change direction. Ask them to run sideways along a line for six steps forwards and then backwards for six steps. Repeat this four times.

(20 mins) Development

Ask the children to dribble a basketball anywhere around the playground, emphasising the ball being pushed firmly to the floor.

Organise the children into pairs, and tell them to chest pass the ball to their partners. Once they have mastered this, ask them to pass the ball to their partners and then move quickly into another space – chest pass and move.

Now ask them to repeat the activity, but this time to bounce pass the ball to their partners.

Ask the pairs to combine into groups of four, and to lay out three cones placed one metre apart. The first member of the team dribbles in and out around the cones, and then runs back to the starting position and passes the ball to the next person. Encourage the children to try to dribble without looking at the ball, and encourage dribbling with left and right hands.

Repeat the activity, but this time, the first member of the team dribbles in and out of the cones and then bounces the ball on the ground past the last cone, then dribbles back to pass the ball to the next person in the team. The game is completed when all the team members have completed the exercise.

Ask the children to get into groups of five, and to nominate one member of their group to be the chaser. The remaining four members are to stand in a circle and pass the basketball to each other, but not to the person next to them (passes must be either chest passes or bounce passes across the circle). The chaser in the middle of the circle must try to intercept any passes. If the chaser intercepts the ball, the last person to pass the ball goes into the middle. Those in the circle are not allowed to move. If after ten passes the person in the middle has not intercepted the ball, someone else becomes the chaser.

(5 mins) Cool-down

On their own, ask the children to walk anywhere in the playground, dribbling the ball without looking at it.

Learning objectives
● Improve dribbling, passing and receiving skills.
● Practise passing and intercepting in small-side activities.
● Practise moving with control with the ball.

Lesson organisation
Classroom introduction; whole-class warm-up; individual, paired and small group activities; individual cool-down; teacher-led classroom review.

Vocabulary
dribbling
shooting
marking
zones
chest pass
bounce pass
possession

Classroom review

Ask the class how the dribbling activity in and out of the cones could be made easier or harder. Can they describe one of the games they played?

Assessing learning outcomes

Are the bounce passes and chest passes correctly performed? How could the shooting skills be made harder for the next lesson? Are all the children in control of the ball when dribbling?

30 mins Can we improve our dribbling and shooting skills?

Learning objectives
● Improve dribbling skills through close control.
● Improve defending skills through good footwork and ball awareness.
● Improve the accuracy of shooting.

Lesson organisation
Classroom discussion; individual warm-up; group activities; paired cool-down; teacher-led classroom review.

What you need and preparation

You will need basketballs (size 3 or 4); hoops; skittles; basketball rings.

In the classroom, discuss with the children the dribbling activities covered the previous week and the key points for success.

What to do

5 mins Warm-up

Ask the children to walk around, bouncing the ball just below hip or waist height, on the same side as the hand they are using to dribble.

Play a number game. Ask the children to dribble the ball in and out, responding to the following commands:
● *One*: dribble and run.
● *Two*: bounce the ball on the spot without looking at it.
● *Three*: dribble the ball and walk.
● *Four*: bounce the ball in control whilst sitting on the floor.

20 mins Development

In a marked out grid, ask each child to dribble a ball. As the children move around, explain that they should try to knock away another person's ball but still keep in control of their own ball. There should be no physical contact.

Ask the children to get into groups of four, and to nominate one member of the group as the defender. A hoop is placed on the ground with a skittle in it. The defender must defend that skittle, but must not touch it or go in the hoop. The other three players move around the skittle, passing the ball to one another. The ball must be passed three times before the attackers aim to knock down the skittle. Discourage running with the ball. The defenders can defend their skittle using any part of the body. Once the attackers have scored three points, a new defender takes over.

In pairs, ask the children to practise shooting into a variety of target baskets laid out in the playground – two teams to a basket. One team watches while the other performs, then change over. Each team has two minutes to see how many baskets they can score. Ensure there is a clear shooting line to aim from. If there are not enough basketball rings, use circles on the wall or on the playground. The team watching keeps the score, the time, and returns the balls to the throwers. Emphasise a two-handed overhead release when shooting for the basket.

Vocabulary
dribbling
shooting
marking
zones
chest pass
lay-up
shielding
attacking
defending
possession

Ask the children to get into groups of four for four-a-side activities. Three hoops should be placed at either end of a grid. In the centre hoop, a skittle is placed. (See Diagram 11.)

The aim is to defend the hoops and skittle as well as attack the opponents' area. Each team is allowed to dribble and pass the ball. Players must defend without touching. One point is scored if the ball is shot into a hoop and three points if the skittle is knocked over. If a team scores, the ball is passed over to the other side to restart the game.

Children can make their own rules to the game (for example the ball must be passed three times before a shot can be made). Play two halves of five minutes each.

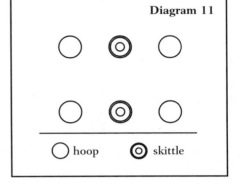

Diagram 11

○ hoop   ◎ skittle

5 mins **Cool-down**
In pairs, ask the children to practise chest and bounce passes.

Classroom review

Ask the children which hoop they defended in the four-a-side game, and why. *How many balls did you knock away when defending your own ball? What was the easiest way to defend your ball whilst trying to knock the other balls away?*

Assessing learning outcomes

How accurate are the children in shooting? Are the children able to dribble and pass the ball with control and accuracy?

30 mins What strategies can we use for attacking and defending?

What you need and preparation

You will need basketballs.

In the classroom, discuss with the children what was taught last week and the expectations for the coming lesson.

What to do

 5 mins **Warm-up**
In pairs, ask the children to label themselves 'A' and 'B'. 'A' runs around the playground with 'B' trying to stay within touching distance. Change after 30 seconds.

Using a netball court or a grid in three parts, put the children into groups of seven, and ask them to arrange themselves one behind another at one end of the grid (see Diagram 12).

The first person in each line runs to touch line A and returns back to touch the next person in their line. This continues until all members of the team have run. When it comes to the first person again, they run to line B. The warm-up is finished when all the groups have run to lines A, B and C. Remind the children to maintain a good running technique.

Diagram 12

C

B

A

**Invasion
(basketball)**

Development and games
20 mins Divide the class into groups for games of four versus three. The team of three start with the ball and see how long they can keep it by dribbling and passing to one another. The other four try to find ways of intercepting the ball. Emphasise that no physical contact is allowed. Change teams at regular intervals.

Then try the activity again, but this time, the team of four starts with the ball, with the team of three trying to intercept.

Ask the children to get back into groups for seven-a-side activities.

The game is played with two teams of seven players. Help the children to position themselves in lines of three and four (see Diagram 13). Three players from each team stand on the end line facing their colleagues. Explain that these three players can only move sideways along the end line. The other four players have to pass the ball to one another and can only score a goal by passing the ball to one of their players on the end line.

Emphasise to the children that the ball must not be passed over head height and that the ball must be passed four times before a scoring pass is allowed. Start the game with a jump ball. Stress that no dribbling or contact is allowed. Change the players on the end line after five minutes, either as a group or one or two at a time.

Diagram 13

Cool-down
5 mins With a ball each, ask the children to practise dribbling around the playground using their right hands and then their left hands.

Classroom review
Ask the children what they felt about the games. Was it easy for a team of three to keep ball possession against four players? Did the games have any effect on their bodies?

Assessing learning outcomes
Do players move into space to receive a pass? How well do players mark their opponents to prevent them receiving the ball?

Vocabulary
dribbling
shooting
marking
zones
chest pass
lay-up
shielding
attacking
defending
possession
jump ball

Striking and fielding

The focus of this unit of work is to look at ways of fielding and batting, and examine specific positions, such as wicket-keeper or backstop.

During learning, the children will need to understand:

● how to prevent a batter scoring when bowling
● how to hit a ball into space and when to run to score for their team
● how to anticipate where a ball might be hit when fielding to prevent a run being scored
● how to throw and catch with good technique
● the importance of using a wide range of shots to score runs
● the need to work as a team
● the importance of applying a range of tactics for attacking and defending, when batting, bowling and fielding
● what strategies, skills and tactics to use to outwit the opposition
● how to identify their own, and other's, strengths and weaknesses and how to improve these areas.

Children should have had prior experience of striking, bowling and fielding individually, with a partner and in mini-side games. The fielding notes on photocopiable page 139 may provide useful reminders during these lessons.

This unit is divided into six sessions allowing 30–40 minutes of activity per session. All the work should be taught in the playground. Many of the activities can be used in any striking and fielding game.

UNIT: Striking and fielding

Enquiry questions	Learning objectives	Teaching activities	Learning outcomes
Can we improve our catching and fielding skills?	● Improve fielding and catching skills.	Warm-up: running around a designated area, responding to commands. Development and games: catching with a variety of balls; fielding in pairs; playing a game incorporating aiming, fielding and retrieving. Cool-down: rolling a ball against a wall and retrieving it; throwing a ball against a wall and catching it before it hits the ground.	Children: ● develop a good technique when throwing the ball overarm ● are effective at stopping a ball when fielding
How do we strike the ball properly?	● Practise striking skills using a variety of bats.	Warm-up: playing a whole-class game turning cones. Development: practising bowling and batting in pairs; playing a mini-side game, bowling and batting. Cool-down: throwing and catching individually.	● bowl accurately ● understand the use of a sideways stance in order to strike the ball effectively ● hit the ball into space ● anticipate where the batter might hit the ball
Can we use strategies to prevent runs?	● Improve the accuracy of hitting a ball into a zone.	Warm-up: running at different speeds in and out of markers. Development: teams of four playing against each other – batting and fielding. Cool-down: repeating the warm-up activity, starting fast and gradually slowing down.	● become more accurate in striking a ball off a tee or when bowled to them ● bowl accurately
When is it best to run?	● Improve batting, bowling and fielding skills.	Warm-up: jogging around the playground; lifting knees. Development: playing a mini-side game involving batting, bowling and fielding. Cool-down: jogging around the playground, then side-stepping then walking.	● make decisions about when to run ● strike a ball away from the fielders ● anticipate when fielding where a ball is going to be hit
Can we prevent runs being scored?	● Score as many runs as possible in six balls.	Warm-up: running around the playground, responding to commands. Development: playing a mini-side batting game, trying to score runs; bowlers and fielders trying to prevent runs being scored. Cool-down: throwing, catching and fielding in pairs; extending catching and fielding skills by delivering the ball slightly away from a partner.	● strike a ball in the air ● stop a ball cleanly ● throw accurately to the bowler ● when fielding, support one another if the ball is hit a long way
Can we bowl accurately, anticipate, and bat in pairs?	● Play and practise a mini-side cricket game.	Warm-up: jogging around the playground; exercising shoulders, hips and legs. Development: playing a mini-side cricket game with four pairs – each pair batting together and everyone taking it in turns to bowl six balls. Cool-down: jogging, side-stepping and walking around the playground.	● aim accurately at stumps ● as fielders, anticipate where the ball is going to be hit ● as batters, work together when deciding to run.

Cross-curricular links
Maths: using addition and subtraction; keeping score.
PSHE: working together, listening and responding to others.

Resources
A variety of bats (padder, cricket, rounders); balls (foam, tennis, airflow); cones; tees; wickets; hoops; photocopiable pages 137–9.

30 mins Can we improve our catching and fielding skills?

What you need and preparation

Make various balls available (for example airflow, foam, tennis) and cones.

In the classroom, discuss with the children the importance of fielding and catching. Ask: *Which games need fielding and catching? Do your parents play any sports that involve those two activities?*

What to do

5 mins Warm-up
Ask the children to run around a marked grid without bumping into each other. On a given command, tell them to get into groups of two, three, four or five.

10 mins Development
With a suitable ball, ask the children to throw the ball in the air, let it bounce and then catch it. Some children might need to use a larger ball to be successful at this exercise if their hand–eye co-ordination is not very well developed.

Ask them to throw and catch the ball in the air without it bouncing and, when they have mastered this, to throw and catch the ball with one hand.

In pairs, ask the children to throw the ball underarm to their partners for them to catch at waist height. If they are struggling with this, allow them to let the ball bounce first before catching it.

In pairs, ten metres apart, ask them to throw the ball overarm to their partners to catch at about chest height.

10 mins Games
In pairs, ask the children to label themselves 'A' and 'B'. 'A' rolls the ball to 'B' who has to stop it and throw it underarm back to his or her partner. After five goes, ask them to change over.

Then ask them to repeat the activity, but this time 'A' rolls the ball to one side of 'B', who has to move sideways to stop the ball and return it with an overarm throw.

Now ask the pairs to stand side by side. 'A' rolls the ball along the ground for 'B' to run after. 'B' runs to the side of the ball and returns it to 'A' with an overarm throw. After three turns tell them to change over.

Now ask the children to organise themselves in groups of six – four fielders, one retriever and one bowler.

Diagram 14

The four fielders stand one behind the other, facing the bowler and behind two cones (see Diagram 14). The bowler rolls the ball underarm between the two cones. The first fielder collects the ball and runs to a cone and throws the ball back to a retriever (positioned to the left of the bowler) who rolls the ball underarm back to the bowler. The first fielder then goes to the back of the fielding line. After three goes each at fielding the group moves around clockwise ('A' becomes the retriever, 'E' the bowler and 'F' lines up behind 'B', 'C' and 'D', who are still fielding). The distance between the cones can be made wider or narrower, depending on the accuracy of the bowler.

(5 mins) Cool-down
Ask the children to practise rolling a ball against a wall and retrieving it. Then let them practise rolling a ball away from themselves, running after it and collecting it before it stops.

To finish, ask them to throw the ball against a wall and catch it before it touches the ground.

Classroom review
Ask the children if they managed to field the ball successfully. Ask: *Which hand did you find it easier to catch with?*

Assessing learning outcomes
Do the children have a good technique when throwing the ball overarm? How effective are they at stopping the ball when fielding?

(30 mins) How do we strike the ball properly?

Learning objective
Practise striking skills using a variety of bats.

Lesson organisation
Classroom discussion; whole-class warm-up; paired and group activities; individual cool-down; teacher-led classroom review.

What you need and preparation
You will need: a variety of bats from padder, cricket or rounders; small balls (small foam, airflow and tennis); markers.

In the classroom, discuss with the children the safety implications of striking. Encourage their understanding that the need to hit into a space must be considered.

What to do
(5 mins) Warm-up
In a marked out area, place a set of 30 markers on the ground. Place half the markers are the correct way up, the other half upside-down. Divide the class into two. Half the class has to put the markers up the correct way, the others have to put them upside-down. The game lasts for one minute. After that, count how many markers are the correct way up and how many are upside-down. Play the game three times.

(20 mins) Development and games
Ask the children to get into pairs and choose a bat and ball to use between them.

In a suitable space, one person bowls the ball underarm to his or her partner who hits the ball back. The bowler needs to make sure that the ball bounces once before reaching the batter. Ask the pairs to swap roles after five goes.

Striking and fielding

Vocabulary
innings
batter
bowler
backstop
wicket-keeper
stance
anticipate

After each child has had several turns at bowling and batting, repeat the activity, but explain that this time, the ball must not bounce before it reaches the batter.

Now ask the children to get into fours, and to nominate one batter, one bowler and two fielders. The batter decides if he or she wants the ball to bounce once in front or not and makes an appropriate decision where to hit the ball. The idea is to hit the ball into a space away from the fielders. A fielder collects the ball and returns it to the bowler. After four goes, change the batter, bowler and fielders.

Still in their groups of four, with one batter, one bowler and two fielders, ask the children to position themselves around a cone (see Diagram 15).

Diagram 15

The bowler bowls the ball underarm and the batter hits the ball, then runs to touch the cone and back to the starting position. The fielders prevent a run being scored by getting the ball back to the bowler who must stand in the hoop. If caught, the batter fails to score a run. The batter starts with ten runs and has four goes. Batters can only score one run at a time (up to a maximum of 14 runs). If they do not succeed in scoring a run after the ball has been hit (that is, they are caught or do not complete the run), then one run is deducted from their score.

Ask the children to repeat the activity in groups of five, with the extra team member assuming the role of wicket-keeper/backstop behind the batter. The rules remain the same except that the batter must run around the cone and back again to the starting position to score a run. Ensure fair turns.

Vary the distance between the batter and the cone depending on how difficult you wish to make the task. The nearer the cone is to the batter, the easier or quicker he will find it to score a run. After a while, encourage the fielders to choose their own positions, predicting where the ball is likely to be hit. However, for safety, make sure they are at least three metres away from the batter.

5 mins **Cool-down**
With a ball each, encourage the children to space out and practise throwing and catching individually. They can use walls to roll or throw against, if practical.

Classroom review
Ask the class if they were successful in striking and fielding the ball. *Did anyone have to change their bat to strike the ball?* If yes, ask why.

Assessing learning outcomes
Is the bowling accurate? Do the batters understand the use of a sideways stance in order to strike the ball effectively? Do the batters hit the ball into spaces? Can the fielders anticipate where the batter might hit the ball?

Striking and fielding

30 **Can we use strategies to prevent runs?**
mins

Learning objective
Improve the accuracy of hitting a ball into a zone.

Lesson organisation
Brief classroom introduction; whole-class warm-up; group activities; whole-class cool-down; teacher-led classroom review.

What you need and preparation

You will need: tees; bats; balls; marked out areas in the playground; 12 cones, other markers or skittles.

In the classroom, advise the children where the playing areas are situated in the playground and who is in each group.

What to do

5 Warm-up
mins

Space out the markers in the playground. Ask the class to form one long line behind you. Lead the class in and out of the markers. Explain that the children must stay close together, without any gaps. Try to vary the speed at which the group travels by putting in short bursts of running and jogging followed by walking. After a while, one of the children can lead the group instead of you.

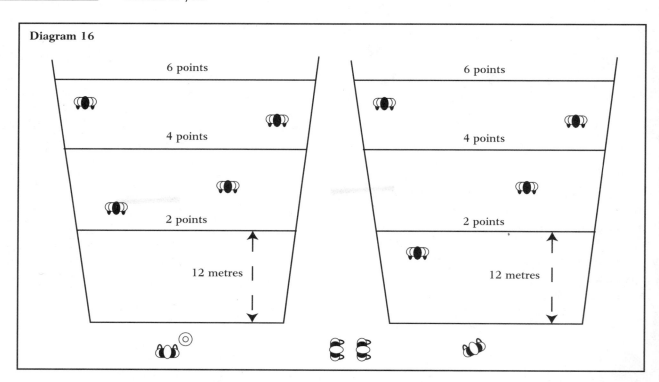

Diagram 16

6 points

4 points

2 points

12 metres

6 points

4 points

2 points

12 metres

20 Development and games
mins

In groups incorporating two teams of four, ask the teams to decide which of them will field, and which will bat. Ask them to arrange themselves as in Diagram 16.

The batting side has four hits each by striking the ball off the tee into any of the zone areas. If the ball is stopped between the 2-point and 4-point lines, the batter scores 2 points for his or her team. If the ball lands and is fielded between the 4-point and 6-point lines then 4 points are scored, and so on. The fielders must be at least ten metres from the batter in front and decide in which area to field in order to stop the ball from crossing the line. If a batter is caught, two points are deducted from the team's score. After each batter has had four hits, the teams should change over.

Then ask the children to repeat the activity, but this time, the batter does not use the tee to strike the ball. The ball is bowled underarm by one of his or her team-mates.

When they have completed this activity, encourage them to try again, using an overarm rather than underarm bowling action.

(5 mins) Cool-down

Repeat the warm-up activity, but this time, tell the children to begin by travelling fast and then gradually slow down.

Classroom review

Ask the class how each team organised keeping an accurate score of the runs. Did each team help by suggesting where and how to strike the ball? How did they decide where to field to prevent runs being scored?

Assessing learning outcomes

How accurate are the children in striking the ball either off the tee or when it is bowled to them? Are the bowlers accurate when bowling the ball to their colleagues?

Vocabulary
on side
leg side
innings
batter
crease
bowler
backstop
wicket-keeper
zone
fielding

(30 mins) When is it best to run?

What you need and preparation

You will need: cricket bats; small balls; markers; cricket stumps; tees; hoops; clearly defined playing areas.

In the classroom, organise the children into groups of eight, incorporating four sets of two ('A' and 'B'; 'C' and 'D'; 'E' and 'F'; 'G' and 'H').

What to do

(5 mins) Warm-up

Ask the children to jog around the playground and, on a given signal, to stand still and perform ten small knee lifts on the spot (five on each leg). Ask them to jog around again and, on your signal, stand still and perform ten high knee lifts, then jog again. Increase the number of knee lifts as the warm-up progresses.

(25 mins) Development and games

In the groups set up in the classroom, ask the children to arrange themselves as in Diagram 17.

'A' bowls to 'B' who has to strike the ball. If the ball is fielded by 'C', 'D' or 'E' in zone 1, the batter scores two runs. If the ball is fielded by 'F', 'G' or 'H' in zone 2, the batter scores four runs. If the ball goes out of zone 2, the batter scores six runs. Each pair has six balls each before changing over. If a bowler hits his partner's stumps, two

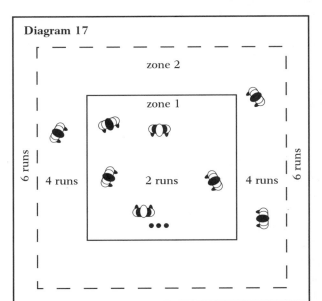

Diagram 17

zone 2

zone 1

6 runs

4 runs   2 runs   4 runs

6 runs

Learning objective
Improve batting, bowling and fielding skills.

Lesson organisation
Classroom preparation; whole-class warm-up; group activities; whole-class cool-down; teacher-led classroom review.

Vocabulary
wicket
stumps
run
on side
leg side
pitch
over
innings
batter
maiden
bowler
wicket-keeper

runs are deducted from their score. If a batter is caught, that team has four runs deducted from their total.

Now help the children to organise themselves as in Diagram 18.

The batter strikes the ball off the tee and runs to the wicket and back again to the tee or stays by the wicket until running back for his next hit. If the batter runs to the wicket and stays there, he scores two runs. If he runs back to the tee without the fielding side placing the ball in the hoop, he scores six runs. If a fielder places the ball in the hoop while the batter is running back to the tee, no runs are scored. The idea is that the batter has to decide whether to go for two or six runs after striking the ball. A decision has to be made between the teams as to what happens if a batter is caught (for example, lose two runs).

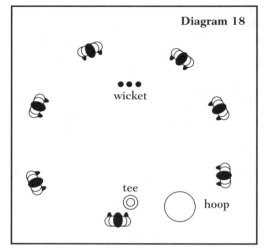

Diagram 18

wicket

tee

hoop

(5 mins) Cool-down
Ask the children to jog around the playground, then side-step for six steps and then jog again. Ask them to walk around the playground then side-step for six steps and walk on.

Classroom review
Did the children work co-operatively? Ask them what influenced their decision to stay at the wicket or run back to the tee.

Assessing learning outcomes
Are all the children able to make decisions about when to run? Do the batters strike the ball away from the fielders? Are the fielders anticipating where the ball is going to be hit?

(30 mins) Can we prevent runs being scored?

Learning objective
Score as many runs as possible in six balls.

Lesson organisation
Classroom preparation; whole-class warm-up; group activities; paired cool-down; teacher-led classroom review.

What you need and preparation
Each group of eight children should have: one cone; one wicket; a cricket bat; a tennis ball.

In the classroom, put the children into groups of eight and organise where each group's area is in the playground.

What to do
(5 mins) Warm-up
Explain to the children that you want them to run around, listening for your call of a sporting discipline. When they hear it, they should respond with an appropriate action:
● *Swimming a width* – breaststroke arm action.
● *Swimming a length* – backstroke action.
● *Hurdling* – jumping over lines on the playground.
● *Football* – dribbling an imaginary ball around the playground.
● *Marathon* – jogging around the playground.
● *Ten-metre sprint* – running quickly around the playground.
Remind the children to look where they are going and be careful to avoid each other.

Development and games

20 mins Ask the children to get into the groups as discussed in the classroom, and to position themselves around the play area as in Diagram 19.

The batter has to score as many runs as possible by running between the wicket and cone. Runs are stopped by the fielders returning the ball to the bowler before the batter has completed a run or runs. If the batter, after striking the ball runs to the cone before the fielders have returned it to the bowler, the batter scores one run. If the batter runs to the cone and back to the wicket before the ball is returned to the bowler he or she score three runs. The bowler can decide whether to bowl under or overarm. If the batter is bowled or caught out by a fielder, he scores no runs, but still has six hits. After six hits, the fielders move around clockwise, with the batter becoming the wicket-keeper.

Diagram 19

Cool-down

5 mins In pairs, ask the children to label themselves 'A' and 'B'. 'A' throws the ball to 'B' who catches it. 'B' then rolls the ball along the ground for 'A' to field. After five goes, ask the children to change over.

Repeat, but this time, 'A' throws the ball in the air but slightly away from 'B' who has to run to catch the ball. 'B' then rolls the ball slightly away from 'A' so that she has to run to stop the ball.

Classroom review

Ask the children which was the easiest way to bowl – over or underarm? Was it more accurate to bowl over or underarm?

Assessing learning outcomes

Do the batters strike the ball more in the air than along the ground? Do the fielders stop the ball cleanly when it comes to them? Are the fielders throwing accurately to the bowler? Do the fielders support one another if the ball is hit a long way?

Vocabulary
stumps
wicket
run
on side
leg side
pitch
over
innings
batter
crease
maiden
bowler
wicket-keeper

35 mins Can we bowl accurately, anticipate, and bat in pairs?

Learning objective
Play and practise a mini-side cricket game.

Lesson organisation
Classroom preparation; individual warm-up; paired within group games; whole-class cool-down; teacher-led classroom review.

What you need and preparation
You will need: stumps; tennis balls; bats. (Kwik cricket equipment is ideal.)

Discuss with the class where the playing areas are going to be situated in the playground. Put the class into pairs with four pairs making a game. Select players on ability.

What to do

5 mins Warm-up
Ask the children to jog around the playground and then work on exercises based on shoulders, hips and legs:

● Circle one shoulder forwards and backwards, then the other, keeping the rest of the body still. Then circle both shoulders, keeping the body still.

● With hands on hips, rotate hips one way and then the other.

● Lift one knee up to the chest and hold the position for three seconds, then change legs. Then lift each leg alternately again, but as quickly as possible.

25 mins Games
Ask the children to get into their pairs as discussed in the classroom, and to organise themselves as in Diagram 20.

Pairs 1 and 3 field, Pair 2 bats and Pair 4 are the bowler and wicket-keeper. Each pair keeps their own score. The bowler in Pair 4 has six bowls and then becomes the wicket-keeper, who in turn becomes the bowler. Each batter receives six balls, and runs are scored by both pairs running between the wickets. No runs are scored if:

● a batter is bowled
● a batter is caught
● a batter is run out before a run has been completed.

Fielders should be at least ten metres from the bat.

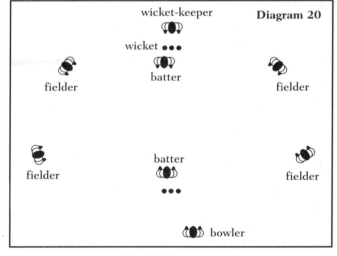

Diagram 20

5 mins Cool-down
Ask the children to move around the playground, first jogging, then side-stepping and then walking.

Classroom review
Ask the children if they all had six strikes each. Ask them where was the best place to field to prevent a run.

Assessing learning outcomes
How accurate are the bowlers when aiming at the stumps? Can the fielders anticipate where the ball is going to be hit? Do the batters work together when deciding to run?

Vocabulary
on side
leg side
pitch
over
innings
bowled
run out
crease
maiden
wicket-keeper
slip

Athletics

It is hoped that children will have had a variety of experiences of running, jumping and throwing by the time they reach this stage of primary schooling, whether as part of the games programme or as athletics in its own right.

The basic skills of the programme – running, jumping and throwing – are essential ingredients of many activities and provide the core foundation for many, if not all, of the physical activities in which they may be involved in the future, both in terms of skill and conditioning.

The aims within the athletics programme are to encourage vigorous activity, personal challenges, beating one's own record and individual progress. Emphasising activity and involvement for all children and allowing as many attempts as possible within the time available will encourage children to strive for improvement, to consolidate their performances and to recognise their own progress. It is important to encourage and recognise optimum effort and co-operation for children to reap the physiological benefits in improved speed, strength, suppleness, stamina and skill.

Children should be encouraged to work together and take responsibility for themselves and others as they discuss, decide and follow the relevant safety procedures for their activities, and help each other as they practise.

The focus of this series of lessons will provide opportunities to help children, whilst practising their running, jumping and throwing, to extend and refine these basic techniques, individually and in combination. Throughout the unit, there is a balance between running, jumping and throwing activities.

The main focus of the first three lessons is on jumping, while in the last three, it is on throwing. Running is used throughout as part of the warm-up activity (with short bursts of exercise and changes of direction). After the main focus of each lesson, the children will be encouraged to practise relay take-over techniques. Details of a selection of warm-up games are provided on photocopiable pages 137 and 138.

Specific ways of throwing different objects for distance will be introduced and various ways of jumping for distance will be practised using a variety of individual and group challenges. This unit seeks to develop children's understanding of how they can improve their performances in these selected activities. They will have opportunities to measure and record their jumps and throws and to take responsibility for different roles within each activity – recording, measuring and organising as well as performing. Where possible, these records can be transferred to computer programs in the classroom. The children will be able to set targets to improve their own performances and help others to do likewise as they develop their understanding of how to improve their sense of general physical and mental well-being.

Each of the six lessons is designed to take approximately 40–50 minutes.

UNIT: Athletics

Enquiry questions	Learning objectives	Teaching activities	Learning outcomes
How far can we jump?	● Practise the standing jump. ● Practise and measure three continuous spring jumps. ● Practise push passing in pairs, gradually increasing the distance. ● Introduce the non-visual take-over.	Warm-up: jogging steadily changing direction; playing 'Chase and change'; stretching. Throwing: in pairs practising a chest pass; moving further away from partner and practising stepping into the push pass and pushing for distance; individually practising the standing jump, trying to increase the distance; trying two to five continuous jumps; practising three spring jumps in pairs. Relay: practising different ways of passing in pairs; practising running in pairs using a check mark. Cool-down: walking quickly then gradually slowing down.	Children: ● work co-operatively and help each other measure fairly ● understand relays
Can we measure a combination of jumps?	● Practise continuous spring jumps or hops. ● Practise and measure a combination of jumps. ● Push pass for height. ● Practise the non-visual take-over.	Warm-up: individually jogging changing direction on signal; playing 'Team release tag' in four groups; stretching. Development: push passing for distance in different positions; practising a standing push pass for height; practising a push pass with a small ball, using one hand; practising several continuous spring jumps; hopping, trying to take the fewest hops to get to the other side; practising three spring jumps and measuring the best jump. Relay: demonstrating and practising the non-visual take-over in pairs at walking and jogging pace. Cool-down: walking quickly getting slower, shaking arms across the body.	● devise a pattern of jumps ● repeat and practise the same pattern ● perform the non-visual relay take-over
What is the triple jump?	● Try triple jumping. ● Co-operate in pairs to organise, measure and record distances jumped. ● Practise an overhead throw with two hands. ● Practise the relay take-over.	Warm-up: jogging moving in different directions; playing 'team release tag' with another group as chasers. Development: practising overhead throw with large ball using two hands; practising transferring weight onto the front foot; determining strongest jumping foot; practising standing triple jump in pairs and measuring best jump. Relay: practising a non-visual take-over at jogging and sprinting pace. Cool-down: walking and swinging, stretching and relaxing arms.	● improve their performances ● perform a standing triple jump

Enquiry questions	Learning objectives	Teaching activities	Learning outcomes
Can we try pull-type throws with one hand and two?	● Practise large strides over a distance. ● Co-operate in twos to organise, measure and record distances jumped. ● Practise pull-type throws with two hands, using a large ball. ● Practise pull-type throws with one hand, using a small ball. ● Practise the non-visual take-over. ● Think about and devise a safety code for throwing.	Warm-up: passing a beanbag in lines of four; stretching. Development: practising 'pulling' throwing action with a partner for distance using two hands then one hand with a smaller ball; in pairs practising large strides; practising and then measuring six continuous strides; encouraging a partner to use his or her arms. Relay: practising a non-visual take-over, introducing take-over zones. Cool-down: walking with a partner, matching strides, changing the length of stride while a partner copies.	● practise and improve the pull-type throw
Can we try a heave-type throw?	● Practise hopping over a distance. ● Co-operate in twos to organise, measure and record distances thrown. ● Practise the pulling throwing action. ● Practise a heave type throw with two hands using a large ball. ● Improve the non-visual relay take-over.	Warm-up: playing 'Exercise detective'. Development: practising the heave type throw over the head with two hands, then one, over one shoulder; practising hops; practising and measuring a standing jump combination and recording results. Relay: practising non-visual relay take-over in fours. Cool-down: individually walking backwards into spaces; relaxing.	● co-operate to measure their best distances ● improve their non-visual take-overs ● understand take-over zones
Can we try a fling-type throw?	● Practise striding over a distance. ● Co-operate in twos to organise, measure and record distances thrown. ● Practise the pulling throwing action. ● Practise a fling-type throw using a quoit. ● Practise and time a non-visual relay take-over.	Warm-up: playing 'Exercise detective'. Development: rolling and throwing a quoit underarm; practising fling throws in pairs; practising and measuring six continuous jumps. Relay: practising a non-visual relay take-over in fours, using circuit. Cool-down: jogging then walking with a partner; shaking and relaxing.	● perform relay take-overs in teams ● manage a fling throw safely.

Cross-curricular links
Mathematics: estimating, measuring and comparing performances.
PSHE: taking responsibility for the safety of themselves and others, observing, measuring and recording accurately and fairly.
Science: appreciating the effects of preparing for and recovering from exercise on the body.

Resources
Chalk; beanbags; tape measures; writing materials; whistle; large and small balls; relay batons; quoits; foam javelins; ropes (optional); cones; stopwatches; photocopiable pages 137–8 and 140–3.

45 mins How far can we jump?

Learning objectives
● Practise the standing jump.
● Practise and measure three continuous spring jumps.
● Practise push passing in pairs, gradually increasing the distance.
● Introduce the non-visual take-over.

Lesson organisation
Classroom introduction; individual and paired warm-up; activities in pairs; individual cool-down; teacher-led classroom review.

Vocabulary
standing start
spring jump
chest pass
push pass
visual take-over

What you need and preparation

You will need: large balls chalk or beanbags; tape measures; photocopiable pages 140 and 143; writing materials; whistle; relay batons or quoits.

In the classroom, discuss with the children the safety procedures for throwing activities and how to measure and record fairly and accurately. Introduce them to the photocopiable sheets and explain how to use them.

What to do

6 mins **Warm-up**
Begin by asking the children to jog steadily around the space, changing direction when you blow the whistle. Emphasise good use of space.

Then ask the children to find a partner and to play 'Chase and change'. 'A' chases 'B', and when the whistle blows, 'B' chases 'A'. Blow the whistle at short, irregular intervals to encourage quick changes of direction. Explain that if the partner is touched before you blow the whistle, the children should immediately change roles within their pairs.

Diagram 1

Ask the children to stretch, holding the positions for the count of five. Particularly teach the calf stretch (ensuring that the children's knees do not extend over their ankles), and stretching their shoulders, with both arms above the head, linking thumbs and pressing their arms gently backwards. (See Diagram 1.)

8 mins **Throwing**
In pairs, ask the children to collect one large ball between two and to practise different ways of throwing to a partner. Then ask them to practise a chest pass, emphasising pushing with both hands behind the ball and following through with arms and fingers towards their partners' hands, at chest height (see Diagram 2).

Diagram 2

Encourage the receiving partners to have their hands ready to receive the ball. As they do, ask them to take a step further away from their partners. How far away from their partners can they get and still catch the ball?

Ask the children to stand further apart (near a line) and to try a push pass for distance towards their partners, emphasising stepping into the pass. Encourage the receiver to let the ball bounce before collecting it. Can they push the ball over the line? Encourage them to take a step further away from the line each time. Practise this several times, before asking the children to return the balls to the baskets.

18 mins Jumping

Ask the children individually to practise the standing jump (two feet to two feet). Ask them what they need to remember to do to help them jump. (Swing their arms and bend their knees.) Then ask them to try to increase the distance.

Ask them to try more than one jump – two, three, then five jumps without stopping in between.

Introduce the three spring jumps adapted from the Ten Step Award scheme. Ask the children to collect their equipment and to work in pairs, taking it in turns to practise the three continuous spring jumps from two feet to two feet. Go through the task from photocopiable page 140 with the children.

Demonstrate that from a standing start, with feet a shoulder-width apart and toes up to but behind the line, the athlete jumps three times without stopping (see Diagram 3).

Diagram 3

Encourage bent legs, a good swing with both arms and a slightly forward lean. Stress continuity. Give each athlete several trials to beat their record and encourage the partners to help each other. Tell the children to help their partners to measure their best jump, measuring from the nearest point on landing (their heels) to the start line. Ask them to record the event and distance on photocopiable page 143.

10 mins Relay

In pairs, ask the children to collect a baton (or quoit) and encourage them to practise passing the baton in different ways, taking it in turns to pass and receive it. Ask them to describe and demonstrate some of the ways they have tried, for example looking, without looking (see Diagram 4), changing hands, stopping, keeping moving. Ask them to discuss some of the things they want to improve if the aim is to get the baton around the circuit as quickly as possible. Emphasise keeping the baton moving quickly.

Diagram 4

Without batons, ask the 'A's to start about 15 metres away from their partners. The 'B's should stand about four or five metres in front of a line, in line with their partners.

On the signal *Go*, tell the 'A's to sprint towards their partners. When the line is crossed, the 'B's start to run and try to reach the next line before their partners touch them. Emphasise that 'B' waits until the line is crossed before running and that he or she must run in a straight line. If 'B' is caught quickly, increase the distance from the line. If she is not caught, shorten the distance or check that she is waiting until the line is crossed before running. Ask each pair to practise this with both of them taking turns in each position and ask them to make the necessary adjustments. It is important for them to practise this ready to transfer the principles to the baton change.

3 mins **Cool-down**
Ask the children to walk quickly around the space using their arms and then gradually getting slower and slower, relaxing their arms at their sides.

Classroom review
Talk about sprint relays. What do the children know about the event? Have they seen any relays? Which relays have they done before?

Assessing learning outcomes
Are the children working co-operatively and helping each other measure fairly? What is their understanding of the relay?

45 mins Can we measure a combination of jumps?

Learning objectives
● Practise continuous spring jumps or hops.
● Practise and measure a combination of jumps.
● Push pass for height.
● Practise the non-visual take-over.

Lesson organisation
Whole-class warm-up; paired practice; individual cool-down; teacher-led classroom review.

What you need and preparation
You will need: large and small balls; chalk or beanbags; tape measures; photocopiable page 143; writing materials; whistle.

What to do

Diagram 5

6 mins **Warm-up**
Ask the children individually to jog around the playground, changing direction when you blow the whistle.

Explain and play 'Team release tag'. With the class in four colour groups, select one group to be the chasers. How long does it take that group (for example, the green group) to tag and stop the other groups? Children from other groups can release those tagged by touching an outstretched hand. If you have time, choose another group to be the chasers.

Ask the children to practise the quadriceps stretch (see Diagram 5) against a wall or with a partner if necessary, emphasising pushing thier hips forward. Then ask them to stretch their pectorals, linking their hands behind their backs and lifting them.

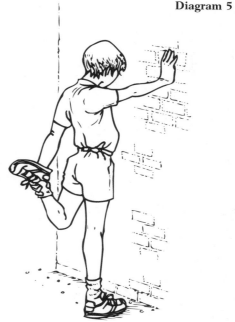

Vocabulary
standing start
spring jump
chest pass
push pass
take-over
hop
stride
jump

9 mins Throwing

In pairs, ask the children to collect one large ball between two and to practise the push pass. If there are some lines on the playground, ask them to take one step back each time and try to push the ball past the line.

Then ask them to try a standing push pass for height, with their partner letting the ball bounce before collecting it.

Ask the pairs to put the large ball away and to collect a small ball between the two of them. (If possible, use a weighted ball or shot.) Ask them to practise a one-handed push pass for height and distance, starting with the ball under the chin. Emphasise transferring the weight from the low back foot to the high front foot.

18 mins Jumping

Ask the children individually to practise linking several spring jumps, with feet together, without stopping in between.

Then ask them to practise several large hops on one leg. Can they get further in the same number of hops if they use the other leg?

Ask them individually to link together two different types of jump and to practise that pattern or combination. For example, hop, hop, stride, stride; hop, stride, hop; jump (two feet) hop, stride; or other combinations, trying their patterns several times.

In pairs, ask them to describe their jump combination to their partners and then help them mark their jumps by placing the mark by the heels of the last step or jump, using a piece of chalk or beanbag for a marker. After several trials, ask them to collect a tape measure and photocopiable page 143 and record their best mark for their combination of jumps.

If there is time, ask them to try each other's combination of jumps.

9 mins Relay

Ask the children to get into the same pairs as they were in for the last lesson's relay, and to practise the same chasing activity.

Demonstrate the non-visual take-over at walking pace, using one pair. The outgoing runner stretches out their left arm behind them, palm upwards, fingers together, but the thumb separated to make a 'V'. The incoming runner, with the baton in their right hand, places the baton down into the upturned hand. (See Diagram 6.) Can the children see a clear 'V' in the hand?

Ask the pairs to practise passing the baton to their partners on the spot, standing one behind the other, with 'A' slightly to the left of 'B'.

Note that the right hand of 'A' should be behind the left hand of 'B'. Then ask them to walk through this action, with the outgoing walker, 'B', starting to walk just before the incoming walker, 'A', reaches her (about two or three metres). As 'A' reaches his partner, 'B' stretches her hand behind her, ready to receive the baton. Emphasise passing from the right hand of 'A' to the left hand of 'B'.

Practise this jogging, gradually increasing the distance covered, and ensure that both partners get a chance to be both the outgoing and the incoming runner.

3 mins **Cool-down**
Ask the children to walk quickly around the space using their arms, then to gradually get slower and slower and shake their arms out as they wrap them around their body and stretch them out to the sides.

Classroom review
Ask the children if they understand the relay and the roles and responsibilities. The incoming runner is responsible for the careful placement of the baton in the outgoing runner's hand. The outgoing runner is responsible for the steady placement of his or her hand (to receive the baton). Ask them to record their pattern of jumps with a partner and to write down the combination and record the measurement. It may be possible to use a computer to do this.

Assessing learning outcomes
Are the children able to devise a pattern of jumps? Can they repeat and practise the same pattern? Are they able to perform the non-visual relay take-over?

45 mins What is the triple jump?

Learning objectives
● Try triple jumping.
● Co-operate in pairs to organise, measure and record distances jumped.
● Practise an overhead throw with two hands.
● Practise the relay take-over.

Lesson organisation
Classroom introduction; whole-class warm-up; paired practice; individual cool-down; teacher-led classroom review.

What you need and preparation
You will need: large balls; ropes (optional); chalk or beanbags; tape measures; photocopiable pages 141 and 143; writing materials; relay batons.
Introduce and discuss the actions required for the triple jump (hop, step and jump).

What to do
7 mins **Warm-up**
Ask the class to jog in and out of the space, moving sideways, backwards and forwards.
Play 'Team release tag', choosing another group to be the chasers. How quickly can they catch and stop everyone?

10 mins **Throwing**
In pairs, ask the children to collect one large ball between two and to practise an overhead throw. One partner practises the throw, with two hands, taking the ball back high above their heads. Emphasise flexed elbows and follow-through, transferring weight from the back foot onto the front foot. Encourage a longer step forward to transfer the weight with the ball kept high, pulled over the shoulders. (See Diagram 7.) The other partner collects the ball and rolls to return it to the thrower. Insist that they change over every three to four goes.

Use lines on the playground or ropes laid out at five-metre intervals as targets to give some indication of the distance thrown. This could be developed by asking partners to place a marker where the ball lands, with the throwers trying to beat their own records and measuring the distance of the best throw on photocopiable page 143.

Diagram 7

Athletics

(18 mins) Jumping

Ask the children to determine their strongest foot by running and jumping off one foot or hopping. The leg chosen would usually be the favoured or strongest leg for jumping and starting.

Practise the hop, step and jump combination. It might help if the children say to themselves, *Same, other, both*, to reinforce the action. Then introduce the standing triple jump from the Ten Step Award (see photocopiable page 141).

In pairs, ask the children to practise the triple jump. Starting with the strongest foot up to the line, the athlete takes off and lands on the same foot, then steps onto the other foot, then jumps to land on both feet (see Diagram 8). Advise the children to have lots of trials and then use a chalk mark or beanbag to mark the distance jumped (nearest point at landing (heels) to the start line).

Ask the children to measure and record their best jump on photocopiable page 143.

Vocabulary
triple jump
hop, step and jump
overhead
transfer of weight
check mark

Diagram 8

(8 mins) Relay

Ask the children to collect a relay baton between two and to practise non-visual take-overs at a jogging pace, taking it in turns to pass and receive the baton. Ask them what they need to try to do to improve the speed and effectiveness of the take-over. (Keep the baton moving quickly.) Emphasise that they should be positioning themselves ready to start the run, watching the incoming runner crossing the check mark, starting to move and positioning their hands to receive the baton.

It is helpful to use a line on the playground (a side of the netball court or soccer pitch) as a marker to indicate when to start running (when the incoming runner crosses the line).

(2 mins) Cool-down

Ask the children to walk round the playground, alternately stretching their arms in the air and then relaxing them by their sides alternately.

Classroom review

Ask the class about the triple jump:
- How did you manage the hop, step and jump?
- Do you know the Olympic champions for this event?
- Do you know how far they jumped?
- How long have women been competing in this event at the Olympics?

Assessing learning outcomes

Were the children able to practise and improve their performances?

Follow-up activity
Children could work in groups on the different types of jumps practised and combine their scores to achieve a group distance pentathlon:
- standing long jump.
- standing jump combination, such as three hops; hop, hop, stride; hop, stride, hop
- standing triple jump
- five continuous two foot jumps.
- six continuous strides (leaps).

(45 mins) Can we try pull-type throws with one hand and two?

What you need and preparation

You will need: a whistle; large and small balls; chalk; tape measures; photocopiable pages 142 and 143; writing materials; foam javelins; batons; cones.

In the classroom, discuss safety elements with the children. Throwing can be a hazardous activity. Ask them to make up a safety code for the activity they are about to do.

What to do

(4 mins) Warm-up

In groups of four, ask the children to line up one behind the other to play 'Pass the beanbag'. Each line jogs around the playground (not crossing any other line) with the front person holding a beanbag. On the signal (your whistle), the beanbag is passed backwards as the line continues jogging until it reaches the back person. That person then sprints to the front of the line to become the leader and the beanbag is passed backwards again until it reaches the new back person, who also sprints to the front. This continues several times until each person has had more than two turns of sprinting to the front.

Ask the children to practise stretching, in particular the hamstring stretch (see Diagram 9), and a shoulder stretch – clasping their hands in front and lifting them up over the head (see Diagram 10).

Learning objectives
- Practise large strides over a distance.
- Co-operate in twos to organise, measure and record distances jumped.
- Practise pull-type throws with two hands, using a large ball.
- Practise pull-type throws with one hand, using a small ball.
- Practise the non-visual take-over.
- Think about and devise a safety code for throwing.

Lesson organisation
Introduction and discussion in the classroom; practice in pairs; paired cool-down; teacher-led classroom review.

Diagram 9

Diagram 10

17 mins Throwing

Ask the children in their pairs to collect a large ball between two, and to practise an overhead throw with two hands. Remind them to transfer their weight from the back foot to the front foot. *Can you throw further than you did last week?* Ask them to use photocopiable page 142 and to record their best throw on photocopiable page 143.

Ask the children to exchange their large balls for small ones, and to try the same action, this time using one hand. Emphasise the pulling action. Can they measure their best one-handed throw? If you have the equipment, try this using a soft foam javelin (see Diagram 11). Can they throw further taking two steps before they throw?

10 mins Jumping

Introduce an exercise of six continuous strides. In pairs, ask the children to practise large strides. Starting with one foot up to a line, the athlete takes off and lands on the other foot and continues striding from one foot to the other, without pausing, to complete six strides. Ask the children to take it in turns and to encourage each other to use their arms, lean slightly forward into the stride and to keep the rhythm of the action. The partner helps to mark the position of the heel of the last stride with chalk or a beanbag. Advise the children not to stop striding too suddenly. Can they beat their record?

10 mins Relay

Ask the children to collect a relay baton between two and to practise non-visual take-overs at a jogging and then sprinting pace, taking it in turns to pass and receive the baton. Make sure that the pairs practise passing with either hand – right hand to left hand or left hand to right hand. Discourage them from changing hands with the baton while they are running (because it takes time, and may be dropped).

Ask each pair to set up two cones about 40 metres apart, and to place two chalk lines (or two skipping ropes) 20 metres apart. Introduce the idea of a take-over zone, and ask runner 'B' to stand four to five metres in front of line 1 (inside the take-over zone) – see Diagram 12. 'A' starts to run around the circuit, and when 'A' crosses line 1, 'B' starts to run and then puts his or her hand back to receive the baton.

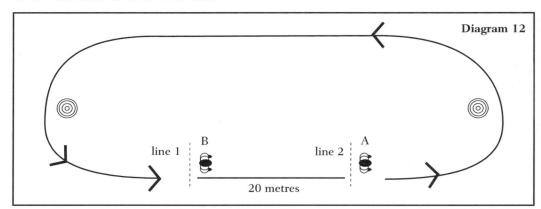

Diagram 12

line 1   B   line 2   A

20 metres

'A' places the baton down into the upturned palm of 'B', ideally at top speed, just before 'B' runs out of the take-over zone (line 2). 'B' then runs around both cones while 'A' repositions herself to receive the baton where 'B' was standing. 'A' receives the baton and runs around both cones to pass to 'B' again. Continue until both runners have had two runs. If the incoming runner fails to catch up with her partner before she runs out of the zone, suggest they stand a little closer to line 1. The adjustments made will depend upon the consistency of the sprinting speed. The idea is not to reduce the speed of the take-over.

(4 mins) Cool-down
Ask the children to walk side by side with their partners and match their strides. Ask them to take it in turns to change the length of the stride while their partners copy.

Classroom review
Discuss the sprint relay with the children, particularly the idea of the take-over zone.

Assessing learning outcomes
Are the children able to practise and improve pull-type throws?

(45 mins) Can we try a heave-type throw?

What you need and preparation
You will need: large and small balls; chalk; tape measures; photocopiable page 143; writing materials; relay batons.
Explain the 'Exercise detective' warm-up activity (see below).

What to do
(6 mins) Warm-up
Remind the children of the 'Exercise detective' activity. (They could work in two groups or as a whole class.) Ask everyone to stand in a circle, and choose one person to be in the middle (the detective). Everyone except the detective decides on one person to be the culprit.

Follow-up activity
Ask the groups to devise an obstacle race that includes a run, jump and throw. For example:
● Run to a cane and cones to do 15 side-to-side jumps; run to a hoop containing four beanbags and throw these into the next hoop ten metres away; run past this hoop to pick up a skipping rope and skip around a skittle or other marker and back to the hoops; throw back the beanbags from the second to the first hoop and run to the finish.
● Jump with feet together from the start line into each of three hoops; giant stride to a marker; collect a beanbag from a hoop and throw it into a bucket; retrieve the beanbagand return to the hoop; run to the finish.

The detective leads the group with an exercise (star jumps, knees up, running on the spot and so on) and everyone joins in. Everyone continues to do that exercise until the culprit changes the exercise. Everyone in the circle has to watch very carefully and change to match that exercise immediately so that the detective has less chance of spotting who changed the exercise. The detective looks around trying to spot the culprit and the culprit waits until his or her back is turned to change the exercise. The culprit keeps changing the exercise until spotted, when she becomes the detective. Ensure that several children have the chance to be the detective.

(18 mins) Throwing

In pairs, with one large ball between two, ask the children to practise the two-handed overhead throw. Making sure that there is enough space, ask them if they can do this backwards, the same distance apart. Standing with their feet shoulder-width apart, ask the throwers to practise heaving the ball over their heads aiming towards their partners.

Encourage them to bend their knees and to follow-through over their heads (see Diagram 13). They could try to mark each other's throws, then measure the best throws and record them.

Ask them to try this with one hand, over one shoulder. Can they try it over the other shoulder?

Diagram 13

(8 mins) Jumping

Ask the children to practise hopping, trying to get across to the other side of the playground with as few hops as possible.

Ask the pairs to plan and practise a combination of jumps (for example three hops; hop, hop, stride, stride; hop, stride, hop, jump). Advise them to record their best attempts on photocopiable page 143. They could demonstrate these to another pair for them to try.

(10 mins) Relay

Ask the children to collect one relay baton between four and to practise non-visual take-overs at walking then jogging pace. Remind them to practise in position, one behind the other, passing from right to left and then left to right.

Encourage the runners to increase gradually the distance between them and improve the speed of the take-overs.

(3 mins) Cool-down

Ask the children to walk backwards carefully into a space, then stretch and relax.

Classroom review

Do the children know which field athletics throws the push, pull, fling and heave are preparation for? (Shot-put, javelin, discuss and hammer.) Discuss the principles of throwing – standing with the forward leg opposite to the throwing arm; starting with their weight on the back foot; transfering the weight to the front foot; starting with legs low, moving forwards and upwards.

Assessing learning outcomes

Are the children co-operating to measure their best distances? Are they improving their non-visual take-overs? Do they understand the take-over zones?

Learning objectives
● Practise hopping over a distance.
● Co-operate in twos to organise, measure and record distances thrown.
● Practise the pulling throwing action.
● Practise the heave-type throw with two hands using a large ball.
● Improve the non-visual relay take-over.

Lesson organisation
Classroom introduction; group or whole-class warm-up; short practice in pairs; relay practice in fours; individual cool-down; teacher-led classroom review.

Vocabulary
detective
culprit
take-over zone

CHAPTER 4
ATHLETICS

Athletics

45 mins Can we try a fling-type throw?

Learning objectives
● Practise striding over a distance.
● Co-operate in twos to organise, measure and record distances thrown.
● Practise the pulling throwing action.
● Practise the fling- type throw using a quoit.
● Practise and time the non-visual relay take-over.

Lesson organisation
Whole-class warm-up; individual and paired throwing and jumping; relay practice in fours; paired cool-down; teacher-led classroom review.

What you need and preparation
You will need: quoits; chalk; tape measures; photocopiable page 143; writing materials; batons; cones; ropes (optional); stopwatches.

What to do

6 mins **Warm-up**
Play 'Exercise detective' with the whole class selecting one person to begin the game as the detective. The others decide on one person to be the culprit and the exercises start. Ensure that several children have the chance to be the detective.

18 mins **Throwing**
Make sure there is plenty of space for this activity. In pairs, ask the children to roll a quoit to each other. Can they start with both feet together and step forward into the rolling action? (See Diagram 14.) Ask the partner to collect the quoit and return it in the same manner.

Ask them to try this for distance, emphasising the flinging action. Develop this by encouraging them to turn slightly to the side, keeping both feet on the floor as the quoit is released (see Diagram 15).

Let everyone practise, and then measure the best throws on photocopiable page 143.

8 mins **Jumping**
Ask the children to practise continuous spring jumps individually. Then, with a partner, ask them to try six continuous spring jumps with one jumping and one marking the landing position (heels) of the last jump. Ask them to take turns to do this, and to try to beat their own record. Encourage them to record their best performances on photocopiable page 143.

10 mins **Relay**
Ask the children to practise the relay in groups of four, around a running track or circuit of four cones. Ask them to decide who starts and who finishes, but to try to ensure that they take it in turns. Use chalk marks or ropes to indicate take-over zones if these are not marked out.

Diagram 14

Vocabulary
spring jumps
continuous
fling

Each team could time themselves and try to beat their own record, or two teams could compete against each other. Try to ensure that these teams are evenly matched.

Diagram 15

3 mins **Cool-down**
Ask the children to jog and then walk around the space with a partner, with one leading and one following. Then tell them to shake and relax.

Classroom review
Encourage the teams to discuss the relay take-overs, what they did that was successful, and what needs more work.

Assessing learning outcomes
How well do the teams perform the relay take-overs? Do the children manage the fling throw safely?

Follow-up activities
● Indoor athletics/potted sports could be arranged as practice or as timed activities: throwing for accuracy – beanbags in the bucket; hitting the target (a hoop); agility run – slalom run; timed shuttle run (time each athlete while running to a marker and back three times); jumping patterns – side to side jump; jump in all the hoops.
● Using the computer to record data, focus on the children setting up, practising, measuring or timing their own performances to improve their own personal best. For example, a shuttle run; slalom run; football throw; three spring jumps, and so on.

Outdoor and adventurous activities

This strand of the PE National Curriculum looks at ways of developing children in their orienteering and problem-solving skills in a variety of situations and environments that are both fun and challenging. Children should be able to use maps and trails, solve physical problems and challenges and learn how to work safely in a variety of terrains. These activities will encourage independence as well as develop personal and interpersonal skills.

Many schools will have access to an outside area suitable for these activities, whether it be a hard play area or grass. In many inner cities there are local parks which will have orienteering trails for schools to use.

For many schools, this unit of work will be covered when going on school journeys. If this is the case, it is the responsibility of the group leader to visit the centre for a risk assessment prior to the trip. The qualifications of the staff who will be teaching the children should be checked, to ensure that they have been appropriately trained through the various governing bodies (for example for canoeing, rock climbing or fell walking).

It is important that you build on the confidence and competence that the children have acquired in their prior learning in the area of outdoor and adventurous activities.

Lesson planning should take into account the balance between the number of potentially hazardous activities that require immediate supervision, and those activities that can safely be allowed with only a minimal amount of supervision. Ancillary help in this area may prove useful. You will need to decide whether warm-up and cool-down activites are appropriate for certain lessons in this strand of the PE National Curriculum.

It is important to check what previous experiences the children have received in outdoor and adventurous activities before planning this unit of work. Previous knowledge might include:

- taking part in simple orienteering trails
- using maps
- working collaboratively in pairs and small groups
- taking part in a range of trust activities
- communication activities.

The lessons in this unit are based on 40 minutes of activity, but in some cases a longer period of time will be required, especially when off site. The best place to start outdoor and adventurous activities will be in the hall, but many of the activities can be transferred to the playground.

You need to ensure that the children have appropriate clothing if going off site, especially if the weather is cold or wet. For any trips, parents need to be informed and the school must ensure that they have the correct adult-to-child ratio as stipulated by the LEA.

UNIT: Outdoor and adventurous activities

Enquiry questions	Learning objectives	Teaching activities	Learning outcomes
Can we work as a team to solve problems?	● Work co-operatively as a team. ● Plan together and acquire leadership skills.	Warm-up: walking, jogging and running around without touching anyone else. Development: co-operating to solve problems using various equipment. Cool-down: creating a dome with a parachute; one half of the class lying under the chute while the other half gently ripples it.	Children: ● work together as a team
Can we trust and be trusted by our partners?	● Develop communication, trust and teamwork skills.	Warm-up: skipping individually and with a partner. Development: building trust and communication skills in activities based on individuals and groups being blindfolded. Cool-down: practising 'mushroom' activities using a parachute.	● guide and support a blindfolded partner ● have trust and confidence in a partner
Can we co-operate to meet challenges?	● Learn problem solving skills. ● Work co-operatively as a team. ● Devise and put into practise a range of solutions to the problems set.	Warm-up: skipping in pairs using one rope between two. Development: carrying equipment over various obstacles in teams. Cool-down: playing a co-operative game using a parachute and a ball.	● know how to lift and carry equipment safely ● recognise the way their bodies worked when moving quickly over an obstacle course
Can we use a map and follow a designated route?	● Introduce orienteering activities related to the class, hall and school. ● Locate a position on a map. ● Follow a route and locate a position.	Development: individually and in pairs, placing and locating various items by following routes.	● orientate a map correctly ● move around safely within the school
How can we improve our orienteering skills?	● Enhance orienteering skills. ● Work co-operatively as a team and as a whole class.	Warm-up: jogging around the playground, sprinting, then jogging again. Development: introducing map-related activities; completing a jigsaw map; filling in a map; finding letters to make words; looking for objects within the school grounds. Cool-down: jogging and then walking around the playground.	● keep to rules ● improve their orienteering skills
How do we use a map and compass?	● Use orienteering and journeying skills within the local environment.	Warm-up: jogging and running for threes minutes around a designated area. Development: using a treasure trail around the local school environment; extending route work to a local park; performing activities using a compass. Cool-down: jogging and walking around obstacles.	● read a map whilst running or jogging ● understand how to use a compass.

Cross-curricular links
Geography: using maps and symbols; understanding compass points.
English: solving problems through discussion.
PSHE: working collaboratively with others.

Resources
Benches; mats; hoops; skittles; crates; beanbags; skipping ropes; mini football goals; footballs with bells in; hoops; gymnastics equipment and apparatus; buckets; water; large containers; a large ball; writing and drawing materials; paper; posts; stickers; aerial maps of the school; maps of orienteering areas; compasses; cards; cones; tape measures; animal pictures; adhesive tape; a parachute canopy.

CHAPTER 5
OUTDOOR
ACTIVITES

Outdoor and
adventurous
activities

Can we work as a team to solve problems?

Learning objectives
● Work co-operatively as a team.
● Plan together and acquire leadership skills.

Lesson organisation
Classroom introduction; whole-class warm-up; group activities; whole-class cool-down; teacher-led classroom review.

What you need and preparation
You will need: benches; mats; hoops; plastic skittles; milk or bread crates; parachute canopy.

For this lesson, the children need to be put into groups of six. The purpose of each activity is to answer the task set by working together as a group. Activities can take place inside or outside. Give each group five minutes' planning time before attempting the task.

What to do

5 mins Warm-up
Ask the children to walk, jog and run around the space without touching anyone else.

30 mins Development
Create a starting and a finishing line. Ask each team to move across the hall or playground without touching the ground in a specific time (such as ten minutes), using three milk or bread crates and two planks. Point out that all the equipment has to pass the finishing line and if anyone touches the ground, the team has to start again.

In groups of six, ask the children to stand on a bench and label themselves from A to F. On a given signal they have to move into the correct alphabetical order without falling off the bench. Variations on the same theme could involve height order or putting surnames in the correct alphabetical order.

Ensure that each group of six has two lightweight mats each. The group must move the mats over a designated area without anyone touching the floor. The group starts on a mat, with the other mat on the floor within reaching distance.

Still in groups of six, ask the children to join hands to make a circle, with a medium-sized hoop on one person's arm. Explain that you want the whole team to climb through the hoop in turn, without breaking the chain.

5 mins Cool-down
Using a parachute canopy, ask the whole class to hold on to the edge of the chute. Ask them to gently lift the chute into the air to create a dome.

Divide the class into halves. Ask one half of the class to lie on the floor while the other half lift the chute over them and gently ripple it. After two minutes, tell the children to change over.

Classroom review
Ask the children how they planned to achieve any of the tasks set. What rules had to be made in order to achieve the tasks set? Did one person end up as the leader in each group?

Vocabulary
problem solving
co-operating
planning
role
responsibility

Assessing learning outcomes
Do all the groups work as teams? Was more time required by each team for planning?

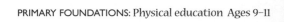

(40 mins) Can we trust and be trusted by our partners?

What you need and preparation

Equipment needed will be: skipping ropes; blindfolds; a variety of obstacles such as hoops, benches, beanbags, skittles, mats, bar box, ropes; mini football goals or skittles; footballs with bells in them; a parachute.

Discuss with the class the importance of working as a team and trusting each other.

What to do

(5 mins) Warm-up

Ask the children to get one skipping rope each and to skip continuously for one minute.

Then ask them to get into pairs, with one rope between two. Let them practise skipping in their pairs.

(30 mins) Development

Ask one member of each pair to put on a blindfold. Explain that the children must be in contact at all times (holding hands or each holding one end of a rope). The person who is blindfolded is taken around the hall or playground by his or her partner. This can be developed by placing obstacles around the floor or ground that the blindfolded child must negotiate with the help of the partner.

Now ask the children to get into threes, with one person in the middle, the others close behind and in front, facing the child in between them. The person in the middle must either keep his or her eyes closed or can be blindfolded, and is gently rocked backwards and forwards by the other two. It is important that the middle person keeps her body tense at all times. Encourage the children to gradually increase the distance of fall before the middle person is caught.

Now ask the children to return to their pairs, again with one of them blindfolded. Together, make up an obstacle course, consisting of benches, tunnels, a section of a bar box, bridges made up of cones and ropes or bamboo sticks, soft play wedges and hoops. The blindfolded children should follow the trail on their hands and feet, with their partners giving instructions on how to follow the obstacle course.

Using the same obstacle course, add a long piece of rope along the ground between and over the obstacles. Keep the obstacles at a low level. If you do not want the blindfolded child to go over any obstacles, then place the rope at floor level around the equipment for them to go around. The blindfolded person is given instructions to follow the rope. It is important that you supervise this activity closely to prevent any accidents. Children who are blindfolded can be set off individually or be tied loosely together in a small group.

Divide the class into groups of six, and blindfold five members of each. Make up goals, either with mini football posts or skittles. Ask two teams of five to play a game of football, using a ball with a bell. Tell the remaining team members to give instructions to their players on when to pass or shoot for goal. Stress that the ball must be kept on the ground at all times.

5 mins **Cool-down**
Using a parachute, ask the whole class to hold onto the edge of the chute and to lift it into the air. Still holding onto the chute, ask them to take one step forwards, bring the chute behind them, and sit on the edge of the canopy, trapping the air inside it, thus creating a mushroom shape.

Classroom review
Ask the children how they felt when blindfolded. Ask them what strategies they used to compensate for being blindfolded when playing a game.

Assessing learning opportunities
How well do the guides support their blindfolded colleagues? Do those blindfolded have the trust and confidence in their 'sighted' colleagues to support them?

40 mins Can we co-operate to meet challenges?

Learning objectives
● Learn problem-solving skills.
● Work co-operatively as a team.
● Devise and put into practise a range of solutions to problems.

Lesson organisation
Classroom discussion; whole-class warm-up; group activities; whole-class cool-down; teacher-led classroom review.

Vocabulary
problem solving
maps
symbols
co-operating
planning
orienteering
role
responsibility

What you need and preparation
You will need: elastic or ropes; hoops; gymnastics equipment (if in the hall) or trees (if outside); planks; various obstacles, including benches, mats, skittles, buckets, water, large containers; a parachute; a large ball.

Make sure the children have the opportunity to solve problems more than once. Encourage them to work in different groups and with different partners. Ensure that all the children understand the tasks and rules set.

What to do
5 mins **Warm-up**
In pairs, ask the children to skip together with one rope between two.

30 mins **Development**
Ask the children to get into groups of six. Make an 'electric' fence, using elastic or ropes and explain that each team has to cross the fence without touching it. This can be made harder by asking each member of the team to carry an obstacle or piece of equipment which also must not touch the electric fence.

Set up a number of hoops suspended between apparatus in the hall or between trees if outside. In teams of four, tell each group to get from one side of the hall or outside area to the other through the hoops, without touching them.

Set up a suitable obstacle course in the hall or playground, at the end of the which is a plank. Organise the class into groups of four and explain that each group has to travel across the obstacle course, without touching the floor, to collect the plank before returning back over the obstacle course to the start. Point out that if any member of the team, or the plank, touches the ground, the group must go back to the beginning and start again.

Set up another obstacle course in which each team of four has to collect eight buckets of water and cross the obstacle course without the water spilling or any member of the team

CHAPTER 5
OUTDOOR
ACTIVITES

Outdoor and
adventurous
activities

touching the floor. Members of the team have to decide what is the easiest way of carrying the bucket (individually or passing it along from one person to another). At the end of the course, the buckets of water should be put into large containers and measured to see who has the most water.

Ask the children to make up their own challenges which involve getting from 'A' to 'B', using a variety of equipment. Each group can plan the course to include restricted areas.

5 mins **Cool-down**
Ask the whole class to hold onto the edge of the parachute at about waist height. Then place a large ball onto the parachute surface, and ask the children to try to roll it round the chute clockwise. Encourage them to see how many times they can roll the ball around the chute without it falling off.

Classroom review
Ask the children what strategies they used to answer the obstacle challenges. What skills were required to answer the challenges set? Did each member of the group contribute to working as a team?

Assessing learning outcomes
Do all the children know how to lift and carry equipment safely? Do they recognise the way their bodies worked when moving quickly over the obstacle course, and does this in any way affect their thinking?

40 mins Can we use a map and follow a designated route?

What you need and preparation
You will need: writing and drawing materials; paper; posts; stickers; a treasure map (see page 116); a parachute.

In the classroom, explain to the children the purpose of the activities and put the class into pairs. Allow time at the start of the session to set up the course and introduce the activity to the children.

What to do
40 mins **Development**
Ask the children to draw a plan of the classroom which includes key features, such as where you sit and where they sit. Ask each child to draw the route from the classroom door to their desk. Encourage them to share their plans or routes with somebody else to check their accuracy.

Go on to ask everyone to draw the route to key areas in the school (such as the headteacher's office, library, computer suite, playground). Again, encourage the children to compare their plans with somebody else's to see if they are the same. Ask: *Are there different routes to key places in the school? Which is the quickest way?*

Learning objectives
● Introduce orienteering activities related to the class, hall and school.
● Locate a position on a map.
● Follow a route and locate a position.

Lesson organisation
Classroom discussion; individual and paired activities; teacher-led classroom review.

**CHAPTER 5
OUTDOOR
ACTIVITES**

Outdoor and
adventurous
activities

Vocabulary
map
orientate
symbol
orienteering
site

Now in pairs, ask one child from each pair to draw a route from the classroom to the playground. Explain that along that route the children should place a number of post sticks, each with a letter on. Their partners then have to follow the route and find the letters which, when put together, make a word (for example *orienteering* – 12 post sticks). Advise the children placing the letters to make sure they are not in the correct order.

Hide ten post sticks around the school that will indicate some form of treasure (for example *gold nugget*). Ask each pair, using a blank map, to find the treasure and mark it on their map. Make a master map for yourself, with all the treasure marked on it.

Together, make a map using a plan view of the hall with all the large fixed and portable apparatus marked on it. Ask each pair to name the shapes on the map.

Ask one member of each pair to go outside the hall, while the other hides post sticks indicating certain types of treasure in more difficult sites, and marks the treasure on the map. Take some time to ensure that the treasure is in the correct place on the maps and then ask the people outside to come in and find the treasure without any form of communication.

Classroom review
Ask the class how they felt the activities went and whether they thought they were too easy or too difficult. *What did you think was the best way to orientate the map correctly?*

Assessing learning outcomes
Do the children have the maps orientated correctly? Are they able to move around safely within the school? Are all the children occupied and on task for the majority of the time?

(40 mins) How can we improve our orienteering skills?

Learning objectives
● Enhance orienteering skills related to the school grounds through running and team activities.
● Work co-operatively as a team and as a whole class.

Lesson organisation
Classroom discussion; whole-class warm-up; paired and group activities; whole-class cool-down; teacher-led classroom review.

What you need and preparation
Find six copies of an aerial map of the school and grounds, stick them onto card and laminate them. Then cut each map into a jigsaw of 18 pieces. Devise a school orienteering map of the playground or school grounds, and ensure that there are enough copies for teams of six to have two copies per team. The first copy should be bare of significant features, and the second will need twelve control points marked on it. You will also need: large paper and a marker pen; tape meaures; paper; writing materials.

Twelve markers such as skittles will be needed. Attach to each of these a letter and a number. The numbers should be from one to twelve, and the letters, when put together, spell out *progressions*.

In the classroom, organise the children into pairs. Ensure that everyone is wearing appropriate clothing for working outside, especially if the weather is cold. Make sure that the children understand the rules for outdoors activities, and that everyone stays within set boundaries.

What to do
(5 mins) Warm-up
Ask the children to jog around the playground. Followe this with a quick sprint and then a jog again.

(30 mins) Development
Put all the pieces of the jigsaws of the aerial map of the school at one end of the playground. Divide the class into groups of six. Explain that each team member must run to

CHAPTER 5
OUTDOOR
ACTIVITES

Outdoor and
adventurous
activities

Vocabulary
problem solving
maps
symbols
co-operating
planning
orienteering
role
responsibility
control point

the far end of the playground to collect one piece of the jigsaw. When they return to their team, the second member goes to collect the next piece, and so on until the team has the whole puzzle. The first team to complete the jigsaw is the winner.

Still in groups of six, give each team the copies of the school orienteering maps. Place the 'blank' map at one end of the playground and the control maps at the other end. Each member of the team has to run to the control map, memorise one of the control points marked on it, run back and draw the control point on the blank map. Each team member will have to memorise and mark on two control markers. When the map has been completed, it can be compared with the control map for accuracy.

Put the twelve labelled markers around the playground (see What you need and preparation). Divide the class into groups of six and allocate each group different markers to visit in order. For example:

- Group A must visit the markers in this order: 2, 4, 6, 8, 10, 12, 1, 3, 5, 7, 9, 11.
- Group B must visit the markers in this order: 11, 9, 7, 5, 3, 1, 12, 10, 8, 6, 4, 2.
- Group C must visit the markers in this order: 1, 3, 5, 7, 9, 10, 11, 8, 6, 2, 4, 12.

Start the groups in different places in the playground. Once a group has collected all the clues they have to find the word by rearranging the letters they have collected (*progressions*).

Now organise the children into pairs. Write out on paper, in large print, ten items to be collected from within the school grounds (for example *something brown* and *something red*). Advise each pair that they can return to the written information if they cannot remember all the ten items to be found.

With a map of the school grounds, mark some features that are highlighted or numbered. In pairs, ask the children to find the items marked and to measure the height of those items. For example, *Estimate how high the school gate or boundary wall is* and *Measure the width of the bench near the wall*.

 Cool-down

Ask the children to jog around the playground and then walk.

Classroom review

Ask the children what they were successful at. Ask them what they found to be the hardest parts of the tasks set. What strategies did they use to conserve energy when tackling the orienteering tasks?

Assessing learning outcomes

Are the activities appropriately challenging for the class? Do all the groups keep to the rules? Were the pairs correctly chosen?

CHAPTER 5
OUTDOOR
ACTIVITES

Outdoor and
adventurous
activities

 How do we use a map and compass?

Learning objective
Use orienteering and journeying skills within the local environment.

Lesson organisation
Classroom discussion; whole-class warm-up; individual, paired and group activities; whole-class cool-down; teacher-led classroom review.

What you need and preparation

You will need: maps marked with routes, compasses; sets of cards with the eight cardinal compass directions; writing materials; cones; paper; animal pictures; adhesive tape; a box.

When going off site it is paramount that the children can be seen at all times. This might entail asking parents to help out at key positions on the trail.

Ensure that the children's parents are aware that their children are going off site and that they are appropriately clothed for all weather conditions. Make sure that you have emergency telephone numbers and a small first aid kit.

What to do

3 mins **Warm-up**
Ask the children to jog and run for three minutes around a designated area.

65 mins **Development**
Ask the children to follow a treasure trail around a supervised route. Give a set of questions to each pair, for example *What is found at the corner of Chrisp Street and Three Colt Street? What date is found on the school building in English Street?*

Plan a circular route in the local park with lots of changes of direction, using recognised paths and different terrains. Along the route, put out six to ten control markers. Ensure the first marker is near the start of the circular route. Explain that on each of the pairs' maps there is a clear route that they have to follow. When each pair finds a control marker, they must plot it on their map. More able pairs can continue on their own while you remain with the rest of the children until they become more confident.

At the end, check all the maps to see if the markers have been correctly filled in on them. With the whole class, walk around the route to collect all the markers.

Give each child a compass and together examine them in detail. Ask the children to draw their compasses and mark in N, NE, E, SE, S, SW and W on their drawings.

Together, use the compass to find where north is in the classroom and then find each of the other cardinal points. Once the children have mastered where the cardinal points are in relation to their classroom, go outside to the playground. Make sure all the children have a card with a cardinal point on it. Demonstrate where north is and ask the children to align their cards to that compass point and then move around the playground to the direction indicated on their card. (The children can swap cards at regular intervals so that they have an opportunity to use all eight cardinal direction cards.)

Vocabulary
maps
symbols
orienteering
compass
route
direction

CHAPTER 5
OUTDOOR
ACTIVITES

Outdoor and
adventurous
activities

Now put out eight cones, spaced out in a rectangle. The bigger the space between the cones, the more exercise the more exercise the children will need to do.

Identify N, S, E, and W cones with the children. Attach a picture (for example a tiger, lion or monkey) to each cone so that routes can be checked. Using three sets of the eight cardinal direction cards, add a travelling action to each card, for example walking, hopping, jogging, skipping and running. Place the cards upside-down in a box. In pairs, ask the children to pick out a card and plot with a compass the direction of the cone they have to find. Tell them to write down the name of the animal they find at each of the cardinal directions. Explain that when they have found the name of the animal, they go back to the start and pick another card. If the children pick the same cardinal direction a second time, ask them to put it back in the box and choose again.

Each group can start from a different compass point (for example pairs A and B start from west; pairs C and D start from south; pairs E and F start from east; pairs G and H start from north compass point).

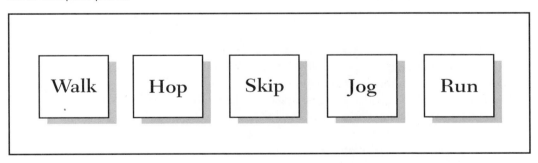

Cool-down
2 mins Ask the children to jog and then walk around all eight cones.

Classroom review

Ask the children if they were able to use the compass. Did they find it difficult to run and remember what to do?

Assessing learning outcomes

Which groups are able to read the map whilst they are running or jogging? Do all the children understand how to use the compass?

CHAPTER 6

Swimming

This chapter will look at developing the work taught in Years 3 and 4 to make the children more competent swimmers. On the premise that all the children have received swimming tuition in the early years of Key Stage 2, the programme should focus on swimming more fluently, improving strokes and learning personal survival techniques. Learning to be proficient swimmers will enable all children to take part in a range of water-based activities.

Where children in Years 5 and 6 are experiencing swimming lessons for the first time and are not very competent, the programme of work for swimming in Years 3 and 4 should be followed.

If you have to teach swimming without an instructor present at the pool, it is advisable to gain an appropriate swimming qualification. In many LEAs, instruction is provided as part of the service and the instructors should have their own lesson plans for teaching the swimming National Curriculum.

Before the class go swimming it is important that:

● any children suffering from an injury or having any physical disability should be brought to the notice of the swimming instructor

● children should understand the principles of hygiene and develop a habit of using the toilet before entering the water and cleaning themselves under a shower if necessary

● the swimming instructor should have written notification of any children with diabetes or asthma and ensure that there are appropriate measures in place on the poolside to cover any emergencies (for example, asthma pumps, a supply of sugar such as a Mars bar)

● you are satisfied that the changing areas for both sexes are supervised, especially if shared with the general public

● you should be present at the poolside whilst any of the children are in the water and, where possible, co-operate with the instructor in the use of group methods of teaching

● you are aware of any LEA rules or guidance on this strand of PE

● you are aware of any rules associated with health and safety, such as the swimming pool's Code of Behaviour.

The school's inclusive policy on integration should reflect all children's needs at any public swimming pool. There should be access ramps for wheelchairs, pool hoists, appropriate changing facilities, correct swimming and buoyancy aids and adequate adult supervision in the water.

In some cases, for cultural or religious reasons, children might be allowed in clothing other than usual swimwear. In such cases, alternative clothing should allow freedom of movement and not seriously affect the child's flotation.

This unit covers the principles of swimming in a large pool. Children should through time know exactly where they are to sit once they are poolside and be ready to be taught.

Where there are swimming instructors present they will have a half-termly or termly plan of work which will include a variety of warm-ups, stroke work, personal survival and some structured activity related to the National Curriculum.

It is important there are at least two lifeguards present during all school's swimming in the public baths. You should be aware where the lifeguards are situated in case they are required. Emergency equipment should be readily available on the poolside to cover any accident.

Knowledge of all previous swimming experience should be readily available. Before teaching any new class, the instructor should quickly test the children to place them in ability groups.

UNIT: Swimming

Enquiry questions	Learning objectives	Teaching activities	Learning outcomes
Can we perform the breaststroke leg action?	● Improve breaststroke leg action.	Warm-up: swimming eight widths of front crawl. Development: using floats, concentrating on leg action; full breaststroke action; treading water; sculling backwards and forwards. Cool-down: performing handstands in the shallow end of the pool.	Children: ● swim breaststroke with the correct leg action ● swim full breaststroke with the correct technique
How can we refine our breaststroke leg action?	● Demonstrate an improving leg action.	Warm-up: swimming backstroke for five minutes. Development: using floats, concentrating on correct breaststroke leg action; swimming widths with correct arm action; swimming full breaststroke. Cool-down: practising straight and star jumps in deeper water.	● make the correct shapes when jumping into the water ● breathe correctly when swimming breaststroke
Can we perform the breaststroke arm action?	● Continue working on correct breaststroke arm action.	Warm-up: swimming backstroke for five minutes. Development: showing correct breaststroke arm action on the poolside; swimming, concentrating on correct breaststroke arm action; swimming full breaststroke with correct leg and arm actions. Cool-down: surface diving through hoops.	● swim breaststroke with the correct arm action ● surface dive through hoops
Can we perform the backstroke leg action?	● Concentrate on the leg action for backstroke, leading to the full stroke.	Warm-up: swimming, using any stroke for five minutes. Development: using floats, concentrating on correct backstroke leg action; working in pairs – one swimming, the other commenting on the leg action; lying on their backs, swimming with legs only; trying full backstroke. Cool-down: performing surface dives, picking up weighted objects.	● pick up objects from the bottom of the pool with the correct surface diving technique ● are streamlined in the water when swimming on their backs
Can we refine our backstroke leg action?	● Improve the backstroke leg action, leading to the full stroke.	Warm-up: swimming either front crawl or backstroke for five minutes. Development: lying on their backs, kicking; using one arm in backstroke action; performing full backstroke action. Cool-down: practising life-saving skills in pyjamas.	● keep their bodies in streamlined positions when swimming backstroke ● tread water efficiently with their pyjamas on
Can we perform the backstroke arm action?	● Concentrate on the arms for backstroke, leading to the full stroke.	Warm-up: swimming choice of stroke for five minutes. Development: holding float in one arm, using the other arm to perform backstroke arm action, changing arms regularly; swimming complete backstroke action. Cool-down: practising life-saving skills, using weighted equipment.	● keep both arms straight as their arms exit the water when swimming backstroke ● pick up weighted objects from the bottom of the pool ● swim through hoops underwater.

Cross-curricular links
Science: looking at forces.
PSHE: appreciating the value of swimming as a healthy activity.
English: evaluating and describing swimming activities and actions.

Resources
Floats; armbands (if necessary); weighted hoops; weighted objects such as quoits, different-sized rubber bricks; toy animals.

30 mins Can we perform the breaststroke leg action?

Learning objective
Improve breaststroke leg action.

Lesson organisation
Classroom discussion; whole-class activities; teacher-led classroom review.

What you need and preparation
All children must have access to two floats each.

Ensure that all the children know where to sit on the poolside when they have changed and know where the swimming aids are placed.

What to do

5 mins Warm-up
Ask the children to swim up to eight widths of front crawl.

20 mins Development
The following activities will help the children to demonstrate the correct breaststroke leg action:

● Holding a float under each arm, with their chins in the water, ask the children to emphasise the leg action with their feet turned out.

● Then, without the use of floats, ask the children to perform the full breaststroke action, using hands and feet. Encourage them to 'draw circles' with their hands along with the correct leg action.

Ask the children to tread water for between three and five minutes, with a modified breaststroke kick or an egg-beater kick. Remind them to control their breathing and scull slowly with flat hands. (See Diagram 1.)

Ask them to scull forwards and backwards on their back.

Diagram 1

5 mins Cool-down
In the shallow end, encourage the children to practise handstands on the pool floor. Get them to lead with their hips, with legs together, as their hands touch the bottom of the pool.

Classroom review
Ask the children how many widths they swam in the warm-up. Did they manage to keep their feet turned out for the breaststroke leg action? Ask the children which direction they swam in when sculling on their back.

Assessing learning outcomes
Are all the children swimming breaststroke with the correct leg action? Are they able to swim full breaststroke with the correct technique?

Vocabulary
front crawl
breaststroke
scull
float
breathe
width
length

30 How can we refine our breaststroke leg action?

What you need and preparation

You will need at least one float per child.

Ensure that the children know which group they are in and where to sit on the poolside.

What to do

5 mins **Warm-up**
Ask the children to see how many widths of backstroke they can swim in five minutes. Remind them to be conscious of where they are going and of other swimmers around them.

20 mins **Development**
Ensure that the children have one float each. Ask them to hold the float under their chin. Then encourage them to swim widths, concentrating on the correct breaststroke leg action, with their feet turned out and their heels down.

Now ask the children to swim as many widths as possible, this time concentrating on the arm action – *Circle with your hands, bring your hands together and push forward.*

Ask the children to swim with a full breaststroke action, concentrating on timing – pull, kick and breathe.

5 mins **Cool-down**
Ask the children to do star jumps into deep water and to alternate these with straight jumps into the water.

Classroom review

Ask the children what is required for a good breaststroke leg action. Ask them what warm-up activities they could use to start a swimming lesson.

Assessing learning outcomes

Are all the children's shapes correct when jumping into the water? Are they able to breathe correctly when swimming breaststroke?

> **Learning objective**
> Demonstrate an improving leg action.
>
> **Lesson organisation**
> Brief classroom preparation; whole-class activities; teacher-led classroom review.

> **Vocabulary**
> backstroke
> breaststroke
> float
> breathe
> pulling
> pushing
> kicking

30 Can we perform the breaststroke arm action?

What you need and preparation

You will need: floats; weighted hoops.

Ensure that the children know where to sit on the poolside.

What to do

5 mins **Warm-up**
Ask the children to see how many widths of backstroke they can achieve in five minutes.

20 mins **Development**
On the poolside, ask the children to demonstrate the correct arm action for breaststroke – circular pulls, bringing their hands into their chests.

> **Learning objective**
> Continue working on the correct breaststroke arm action.
>
> **Lesson organisation**
> Brief classroom preparation; whole-class activities; teacher-led classroom review.

Swimming

Vocabulary
backstroke
breaststroke
surface dive

With full breaststroke action, ask the children to perform the following tasks:
● swim as many widths as they can in *eight* minutes, concentrating on keeping their arms in line with their shoulders, with small pulls
● swim as many widths as they can in *eight* minutes, concentrating on small circles with their hands.
● swim as many widths as they can in *four* minutes, with both the correct leg and arm actions.

⑤ Cool-down
mins Put weighted hoops at various depths in the pool. Encourage the children to choose a hoop and swim towards it, then surface dive to swim through it, come to the surface and swim on to another hoop to do the same. Encourage them to try both head-first (see Diagram 2) and feet-first (see Diagram 3) surface dives.

Diagram 2   **Diagram 3**

Classroom review
Ask the children to describe how swimming affects different parts of the body, including the heart and lungs. Ask them why swimming is good exercise to improve their fitness and health. Can they describe what makes a good breaststroke action?

Assessing learning outcomes
Are all the children able to swim breaststroke with the correct arm action? Are they able to surface dive through the hoops?

(30 mins) Can we perform the backstroke leg action?

What you need and preparation

Discuss with the children the key points of what is to be taught for the backstroke.

Once at the pool, ask the children to sit in their ability groups on the poolside with one float each. The children will also need rubber bricks and weighted rings or quoits.

Learning objective
Concentrate on the leg action for backstroke, leading to the full stroke.

Lesson organisation
Classroom introduction; whole-class and paired activities; teacher-led classroom review.

What to do

(5 mins) Warm-up
Ask the children to see how many widths they can swim on their front in five minutes, using any stroke.

(20 mins) Development
Ask the children to lie their backs, holding a float across their chests with both hands, and to swim as many widths as they can using only their legs in five minutes. Encourage everyone to concentrate on keeping pointed toes.

Tell the children to get into pairs, and ask one partner to swim two widths while the other observes and then feeds back on how the leg action could be improved. Then ask the children to change roles.

Vocabulary
backstroke
breaststroke
surface diving

Now instruct everyone to lie their backs with their arms by their sides, and to swim using their legs only. Encourage them to keep their tummies pushed up, with their legs straight and their toes pointed.

Ask the children to perform the full backstroke action with fast leg kicks (see Diagram 4).

Diagram 4

(5 mins) Cool-down
Place a number of objects, such as rubber bricks or rings at different depths of the pool. Encourage the children to swim over the objects, surface dive to pick them up and then swim on to place the objects on the poolside.

Classroom review

Ask the children how many objects they picked up from the bottom of the pool. Discuss what is required for a good leg action when swimming backstroke. Ask them to identify aspects of their work that need improvement and suggest ways to practise them.

Assessing learning outcomes

Are the children able to pick up the objects from the bottom of the pool with the correct surface diving technique? Are they streamlined in the water when swimming on their backs?

30 mins Can we refine our backstroke leg action?

What you need and preparation

The children will need to bring their pyjamas.

Review the last lesson on the leg action for backstroke. Ensure that the children know where to sit for the start of the lesson.

What to do

5 mins Warm-up

Ask the children to choose between the front crawl (see Diagram 5) and backstroke to warm up with. Encourage them to see how many widths they can achieve in five minutes using the correct breathing technique and good arm and leg actions.

20 mins Development

Ask the children to lie on their backs with the body streamlined on top of the water, and with their hands by the side of their bodies. Encourage them to keep their legs stretched and toes pointed, and to kick their legs to propel them backwards.

Now ask them to repeat the action, but this time with only one arm remaining by their sides. Explain that the other arm should come out of the water as straight as possible and cut into the water with the little finger entering first. Ask the children to change arms after two widths.

Invite the children to swim full backstroke, concentrating on fast leg kicks and a slow, long arm action.

5 mins Cool-down

Ask the children to wear pyjamas to practise swimming with their clothes on as part of their personal life-saving skills, including treading water.

Classroom review

Ask the children what effect wearing clothes to swim in had on their bodies. Ask them to describe certain parts of the backstroke action.

Assessing learning outcomes

Are all the children able to keep their body in streamlined positions when swimming backstroke? Are they able to tread water efficiently while wearing their pyjamas?

Diagram 5

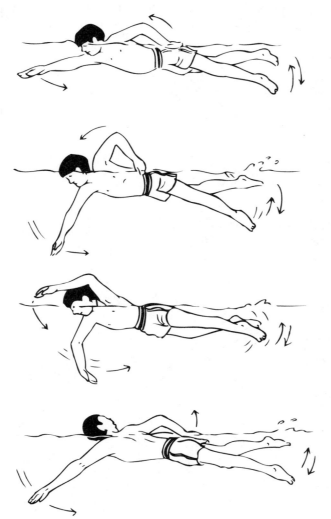

(30 mins) Can we perform the backstroke arm action?

What you need and preparation
You will need a float for each child; weighted hoops; a variety of weighted objects and different-sized rubber bricks for life-saving practice.

Discuss with the class what warm-up activities they will be using to start off the swimming lesson. Ensure that the children know where to sit when they get to the pool.

What to do

(5 mins) Warm-up
Ask the children to choose their own stroke and see how many widths they can achieve in five minutes.

(20 mins) Development
Ask the children to hold a float with one arm across their chests whilst lying on their backs. With a fast leg action, encourage them to bring the other arm out of the water in a straight line, with their little finger entering the water first.

Ask them to repeat this, changing the arm holding the float.

Then ask them to repeat it again, this time changing the arm holding the float after each width. Make sure that they push their hands to the sides of their bodies before their hands come out of the water.

Now tell the children to swim the complete stroke, concentrating on the correct arm action. Remind them that as one straight arm enters the water, the other arm starts to move out.

(5 mins) Cool-down
Ask the children to choose an aspect of their life-saving skills to practise, involving weighted hoops, weighted quoits, toy animals and rubber bricks.

Classroom review
Ask the children which aspect of their survival skills they were proficient in. Ask them which arm they favoured when swimming the backstroke (this should be the right arm if right-handed, left arm if left-handed).

Assessing learning outcomes
When swimming backstroke, do the children keep both arms straight as their arms exit the water? How many weighted objects did each child pick up? Are all the children able to swim through the hoops?

Learning objective
Concentrate on the arms for backstroke, leading to the full stroke.

Lesson organisation
Classroom discussion; whole-class activities; teacher-led classroom review.

Vocabulary
front crawl
backstroke
breaststroke
surface diving
life-saving

PHOTOCOPIABLE

DANCE: **Dances from history**
What are the polka and the pavan? Page 13

Elizabethan costume

DANCE: *Oliver Twist*
Can we stroll, swagger, dodge and creep? Page 30

PHOTOCOPIABLE

Walking

The End of the Road

In these boots and with this staff
Two hundred leagues and a half
Walked I, went I, paced I, tripped I,
Marched I, held I, skelped I, slipped I,
Pushed I, panted I, swung and dashed I;
Picked I, forded, swam and splashed I,
Strolled I, climbed I, crawled and scrambled,
Dropped and dipped I, ranged and rambled;
Plodded I, hobbled I, trudged and tramped I,
And in lonely spinnies camped I,
Lingered, loitered, limped and crept I,
Clambered, halted, stepped and leapt I,
Slowly sauntered, roundly strode I,
And…
Let me not conceal it …rode I.

Hilaire Belloc

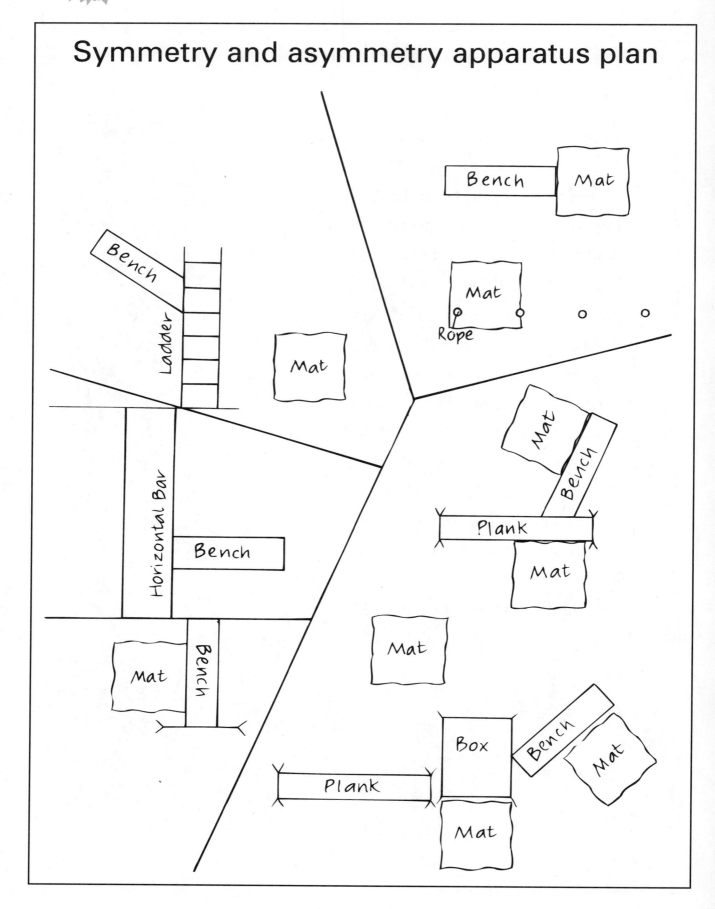

Symmetry and asymmetry apparatus plan

Ideas for symmetry

Ideas for asymmetry (1)

Ideas for asymmetry (2)

Symmetry

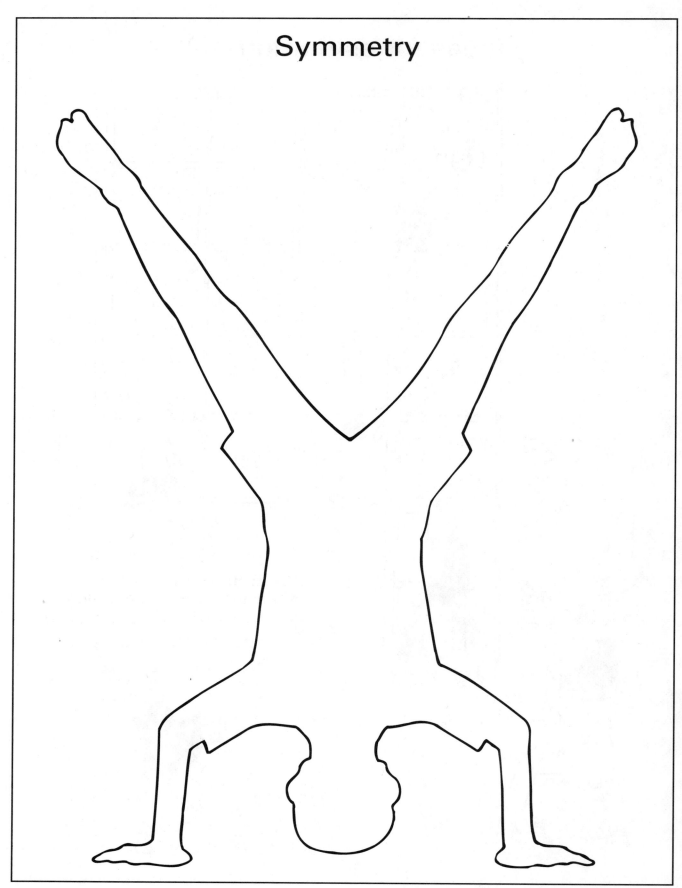

Gymnastic skills – rolling

Sideways shoulder roll
● If rolling to the *left*, roll across your shoulder, over your bent leg.
● Drop the leading shoulder to start the movement, which should be smooth and

Forward roll
● Use a rocking action.
● Keep a tight tucked shape, with your chin on your chest.
● Your knees should be on your chest and your heels by your bottom when you are rocking towards the floor.

Rock to stand
● Use a rocking action, but stand up, with feet together if possible.
● Reach forward to move into a standing position.

Forward roll to long sit (or stand)
● Ensure your hips are high.
● Roll across your shoulders in a tucked shape, lowering to a sitting position.

Starting a forward roll in different ways

Using a forward roll in a movement phrase

Ideas for counterbalance

Warm-up games (1)

Chase and change

In pairs, ask 'A' to chase and try to touch 'B'. Blow the whistle as a signal to change over so that 'B' chases 'A'. Blow the whistle at short, irregular intervals to encourage quick changes of direction. If the partner is touched before the whistle blows, the children immediately change roles.

Team release tag

With the class split into four colour-coded groups, select one group to be the chasers. How long does it take that group to stop the other groups? Children from other groups can release those tagged by touching an outstretched hand. If time is available, rotate the groups.

Pass the beanbag

In groups of four, ask the children to line up behind each other. Each line jogs around the space (not crossing any other line), with the front person holding a beanbag. On a given signal (such as a whistle blow), the beanbag is passed backwards as the line continues jogging, until it reaches the back person. That person then sprints to the front of the line to become the leader. This continues several times until each person has had more than two turns of sprinting to the front.

Warm-up games (2)

Beanbag thief

Put the children into four colour-coded groups and ensure that there are four hoops and 16 beanbags available. Place the hoops (to be the groups bases) in opposite corners of the space, and four beanbags within each hoop. On your signal, the children must run to another group's home base to steal *one* beanbag to store in their own hoop. No one is allowed to stay and guard the home base. On a signal, such as *Stop* or *Freeze*, the children must freeze, and the number of beanbags in each home base are counted.

Exercise detective

This could work as an activity for two groups, or for the whole class.

Ask everyone to stand in a circle and to choose one person to be in the middle (the detective). Everyone except the detective then decides on one person to be the culprit. The detective leads the group with an exercise (for example star jumps, knees up, running on the spot, press ups) and everyone joins in. Everyone continues to do that exercise until the culprit changes it.

Explain that everyone in the circle has to watch very carefully and change to match that exercise immediately so that the detective has less chance of spotting who changed the exercise. The detective looks around trying to spot the culprit and the culprit waits until the detective's back is turned to change the exercise. The culprit keeps changing the exercise until spotted, when she becomes the detective.

Ensure that several children have the chance to be the detective.

Fielding skills

Points for catching
● Watch the ball whilst it is in the air.
● Get underneath the ball if it is high in the air.
● Move your feet and body to get into the direct path of the ball.
● Make a cup shape with your hands (fingers upwards) to receive the ball.
● Make a cup shape with your fingers downwards to catch a low ball.
● Squeeze the ball tightly and pull it in towards your chest.

Throwing overarm
● Hold the ball between your thumb and first two fingers.
● If *right* handed, plant your left leg forward and hold your left arm forward.
● Reach your right hand behind your head and well away from your body.
● Use your left arm to 'point' at the target.
● Throw the ball with a snapping action through your elbow, wrist and fingers.
● Follow through with your throwing arm straight.

Intercepting and fielding
A ball running away from you
● Run alongside the ball before it stops rolling.
● Bend your knees and use one hand to pick up the ball (with your fingers towards the ground).
● Turn, and return the ball to the wicketkeeper or bowler.

A ball coming towards you
● Get into a barrier position.
● Place one knee on the ground, next to the heel of your other foot, with your body at a right angle to the ball.
● Put your hands in a cradle position, fingers facing down, to receive the ball.
● Pick the ball up cleanly and return it with an overarm action.
● If your hands miss the ball, your legs or body will stop it.

A ball rolling to one side of you
● Watch the ball carefully.
● Run to get into the pathway of the ball.
● Adopt a barrier position to receive the ball (as above).

Three spring jumps

Equipment: chalk to mark the distance; a tape measure to measure the best longest jump.

Task: Three continuous jumps from a standing start.

● Start with feet together behind the take-off line and jump three times, landing on two feet.

● Practise several times and mark the distance each time.

● Measure and record the best jump from the nearest point at landing (heel mark) to the start line.

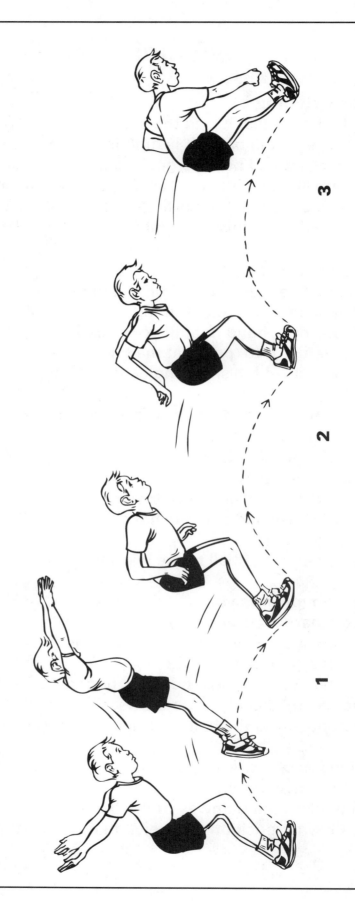

1   2   3

Adapted from the Ten Step Award

Teaching points: Look for a continuous action with an equal emphasis on each jump and a forward arm swing on each landing. Stress that the child swings his or her arms forward on each landing.

Standing triple jump

Equipment: chalk to mark the distance; a tape measure.

Task: Hop, step and jump from a standing start.
● Start with the strongest foot just behind the take off line. **Hop** (landing on the take-off foot), **step** (onto the other foot) and **jump** (landing on two feet).
● Measure and record the furthest jump from the nearest point at landing (heel mark) to the start line.

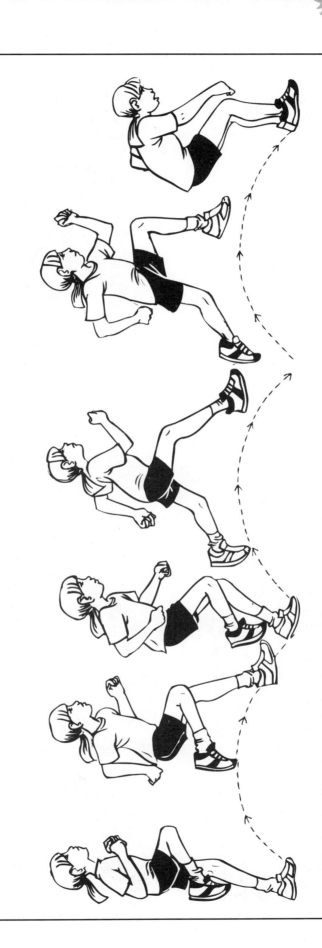

Adapted from the Ten Step Award

Teaching points: Look for flat-foot landings and a continuous action with equal emphasis on each phase. Encourage the child to use his or her arms to assist each phase.

PHOTOCOPIABLE

ATHLETICS
Can we try pull-type throws with one hand and two? Page 104

Standing overhead throw

Equipment: 1 football (size 4) between two; chalk or a beanbag to mark where the ball lands; a tape measure for the longest throw.

Task: See how far you can throw.
● In a large space, start with the ball behind your head, one foot in front of the other.
● ● Practise throwing, with both hands, several times.
● Measure and record your best distance.

Teaching points: Look for good feet positioning (one foot in front of the other) and spread, and the transfer of weight from back to front. Advise the child to use a big lean back and then to follow through. Remind him or her to keep both hands on the ball until release.

Adapted from the Ten Step Award

Name

Record sheet

Event	Distance						Best performance

Swimming dos and don'ts

At school, children should:
● know on what day they will be swimming
● check that they have all the appropriate swimwear, such as costume, swimming hat, goggles and towel
● have the correct money for lockers if necessary.

At the pool, children should:
● change tidily and quickly
● organise their clothing in an appropriate place in the changing area or cubicle, or in a locker
● wear appropriate clothing for the lesson
● go to the toilet before the start of the lesson, ideally before changing
● use the footbath or shower before going to the poolside
● not chew gum during the lesson
● remove any jewellery
● put any asthma inhalers in a safe place near the pool
● walk in an orderly fashion to the poolside.

At the poolside, children should:
● know where to sit in their ability groups
● know where equipment, such as armbands and floats, is placed for use during the lesson
● avoid pushing and splashing
● enter and swim, showing consideration for others
● be aware of the pool's emergency policies
● know how to deal with an emergency situation that could arise
● leave the pool in an orderly fashion after the lesson.

At the pool, you should:
● supervise the children while changing
● ensure that any child with a medical condition or disability is known to the instructor
● ensure that children with asthma bring their inhalers
● be on the poolside at all times, either supporting the instructor or monitoring the class
● make sure that any children not participating are appropriately situated, with work to do
● avoid walking on the poolside with outdoor shoes.